Praise for *When Justice Just Is*

"Katie has bravely invited us into the fabric of her soul. And through this book she has quenched the thirst of the wandering humanitarian. We beg for a voice that relinquishes us from the weight of helping and she has challenged us to find beauty and rest amongst the thorns of working for justice. Katie's journey gives us permission live justly while living well and the community is empowered to live beautifully. This is a message for every worker of justice."

—Ginger Coakley, CEO of Eden's Glory and Regional Director for the Set Free Movement www.edensglory.org

"*When Justice Just Is* is an engaging and well-crafted personal memoir of Katie Bergman's journey from innocent naiveté through disillusionment to a more realistic or "tempered idealism" in the world of non-profits and charities that seek to "do justice" in the world today. The author has a gift for striking turns of phrase and evocative anecdotes, and for discerning "life lessons" from her experiences. But the book is more than just a personal memoir; it is also a compelling analysis, perhaps even exposé, of the way charity and charitable institutions operate unjustly through glamorous marketing, imposed handouts and inducement of "compassion fatigue" and "martyr complexes". The author's call for balance, acceptance of failure, a long-term view, and hope and compassion applied to one's self as well as to the world, provides both personal and institutional guidelines for a more humane humanitarianism. This book deserves to be read for its compelling narrative and for the benefit of those who run non-profits and charities, those who work for them, and those who fund them."

—F. Volker Greifenhagen, Academic Dean and Professor of Religious Studies at Luther College, University of Regina

"This book gave me a glimpse into the soul of a hungry, passionate woman who sensed early on in her life that she was meant to love the world. On her journey of seeking freedom and justice for others, Katie discovered her own freedom and well-being matters too. What moved me most, was when Katie recognized how seeking justice is very similar to the summers she spent planting trees in Northern British Columbia: how we need to trust that the small seed we plant in our work will be enough. This book was refreshingly honest and an inspiring read with a good shot of realism for anyone who longs to make a difference in the world."

—Idelette McVicker, Founder and Editor-in-Chief of SheLoves Magazine.com
www.shelovesmagazine.com

"This is THE book I wish I would have read at the beginning of my career. After twenty-two years in the human rights field, I was touched and outraged and humbled by Katie's experiences and her straight-from-the-heart words. She gets to the soul of what many of us feel, but few say. This book is for everyone who yearns to make changes in the way we do charity."

—Jill Morris, Victims Rights Advocate and Field Liaison for the NO MORE Campaign

"From the wilderness of the Canadian prairies, to the dusty, dirt-filled streets of Poipet, to the deserts of Mexico comes a powerful new voice in the social justice field. Katie Bergman's *When Justice Just Is* is a compelling read for activists, abolitionists, idealists, and realists alike. Through personal stories and reflections, Katie details her struggle with justice. She describes the vividly known, yet all too often hidden tension between doing what is right and what is just, between justice and mercy, and between charity and compassion. Katie's voice echoes with a bittersweet vulnerability that is not overshadowed by her tenacious resilience or generosity of spirit."

—Keturah Lee Schroeder, Community Support Coordinator for CATCH Court—a restorative justice program for victims of human trafficking and prostitution in Ohio

"Justice has been trendy for some time now. At least, talking about causes and dipping our toes in has become trendy. Somehow, though, we've managed to make it about ourselves—Katie Bergman calls it a "virtuous veneer" in this book. With wisdom beyond her years, Katie lifts the romanticized veil we often layer on top of humanitarian work and shatters the idea of justice as an easy, feel-good experience. With vulnerability, she tells the truth about her own difficult and often discouraging experiences in humanitarian pursuits around the world, and she shares her own process of moving through disillusionment and coming out on the other side to find realistic hopefulness. *When Justice Just* is a book for anyone who is experiencing their own disillusionment and looking for a way to hold onto hope without letting go of reality."

—Beth Clayton Luthye, Anti-Trafficking Coordinator and Communications Manager, Nazarene Compassionate Ministries
www.ncm.org

"With confessional storytelling and spirited candor, Katie speaks to the human in every humanitarian. She takes you around the globe into her experiences, sharing the discoveries and disillusionment of meeting justice on its own terms. Through the pages, I was endeared to her story, contemplative of my own journey, and convicted by her corrective challenges. As she confronts the influence of our romanticized projections, expectations and marketing, she offers space where we can also examine our own attachment with our work. She gives voice to a rare but needed conversation that while still infused with hope, invites greater honesty, reflection and wisdom into the discussion of what it looks like to sustain a life of authentic advocacy."

—Kelly Grace, M. Div, MFT, Street Pastor and Director of Set Free Movement Oregon
www.setfreemovement.org

"Most people I know who are invested into the work of impacting sustainable change in this world often end up moving on to something easier because the price is just too great to pay over a life-time of serving. The needs are great, our passions are strong, and our enthusiasm is high. However, those things will not sustain us over a lifetime of service. In writing *When Justice Just Is*, Katie has given world-changers a clear path to a balanced, sustainable life, both personally and professionally. This book will help keep generations of world-changers in the game, instead of tapping out because the struggle is too great. If you are a veteran difference-maker or someone just exploring this way of life, this book might just help save your life...and the lives of the people you serve."

—Tim Coleman, Founder and Lead Pastor at Brown's Mill Church

WHEN **JUSTICE JUST** IS

Confessing Brokenness, Cultivating Joy,
and Creating Space for Authenticity
in the Justice Movement

KATIE BERGMAN

WESTBOW
PRESS®
A DIVISION OF THOMAS NELSON
& ZONDERVAN

WestBow Press books may be ordered through
booksellers or by contacting:

WestBow Press
A Division of Thomas Nelson & Zondervan
1663 Liberty Drive
Bloomington, IN 47403
www.westbowpress.com
1 (866) 928-1240

Because of the dynamic nature of the Internet, any web addresses or
links contained in this book may have changed since publication and may
no longer be valid. The views expressed in this work are solely those
of the author and do not necessarily reflect the views of the publisher,
and the publisher hereby disclaims any responsibility for them.

Any people depicted in stock imagery provided by Thinkstock are
models, and such images are being used for illustrative purposes only.
Certain stock imagery © Thinkstock.

ISBN: 978-1-5127-1271-1 (sc)
ISBN: 978-1-5127-1272-8 (hc)
ISBN: 978-1-5127-1270-4 (e)

Library of Congress Control Number: 2015915135

Print information available on the last page.

WestBow Press rev. date: 11/06/2015

To my parents,
the first two people to see the writer in me,
the first ones to encourage me
to write this book in the first place

CONTENTS

Part III. Living Beautifully

FOREWORD

By Kevin Austin, Set Free Movement

I remember like it was yesterday standing on the Thai side of the border between Thailand and Burma and watching a young girl begging in Burma. As I watched, the girl became more and more frantic. It was incredibly painful to watch knowing that I was completely helpless to do anything. If I could do something, what would I do? For many nights she haunted my dreams.

Too often our first response to the problems we experience is to ask *what* can be done? *What* should I do? The question is a natural one. Unfortunately, the questions concerning *how* best to respond and *why* we are compelled to respond go unasked and therefore unanswered. The result of only dealing with the first question is that we end up doing some valuable things, but sometimes also terrible things. Any means to reach an end based on faulty understandings, quick judgments, and overly charged emotions perpetuate the brokenness because the *how* and *why* are just as important as the *what*.

Katie Bergman challenges not just the *what*, but probes deep into the questions of *how* and *why*. Her voice is prophetic in that she wakes us up and helps us see the pursuit of justice in new, sometimes painful, yet ultimately hopeful ways. Her insights are keen and her wisdom is deep. We need to listen to this voice, this call to pursue justice in a holistic way, balancing community and action.

Katie calls us to community. She invites us to pursue justice with humility and grace, beauty, and hope. Within the lines of the book she implies that injustice is not something "out there," separate from us and therefore something we fight against. No. Injustice comes from our own brokenness. Therefore, *how* we go about engaging in serving the marginalized and *why* we do what we do is just as much as part of the solution as numbers, programs, and projects.

Personally, as a leader who works with young, emerging leaders, I'll be handing this book out regularly. It's vitally important that we curb the triumphalism and glamor associated with fighting injustice. Also, as a director of a non-profit I'm once again convicted that how I treat all who work for and with my organization and me matters. Respect and dignity, humility, grace, and hope must rule.

As you read this book be prepared to stop mid paragraph and think deeply. Be open to conviction. Have your pen ready to mark things up. But don't just read this book. Be changed by it.

Kevin Austin
Director, Set Free Movement
www.setfreemovement.org

AUTHOR'S NOTE

Two wise people once told me a long time ago that loving others comes more naturally when I love myself. *Easier said than done*, I'd always tell myself. Or, *I'll love myself when I have more time to work on that*. The profundity of the thought of loving myself now as I am didn't hit me until more recent years. It was when every piece of myself—body, mind, and soul— became engrossed in justice pursuits that I started realizing how hard it was to help others when I didn't treat myself with the same love, respect, and boundaries. Their needs always seemed to matter more than mine. I believed their intrinsic value had more worth than my own.

I don't have it all figured out yet, nor do I ever expect myself to fully understand. But through a series of experiences that turned my world upside down—some of which I share in this book—I'm starting to learn to think differently and live differently, too. I'm starting to find less guilt, more joy, and better daily living in being okay with allowing myself to be imperfect: as a director at a non-profit and as a humanitarian, as a writer and as an adventurer, as a sister and friend and daughter.

One of the most meaningful ways I've been able to look at human flourishing is through a quote credited to Socrates: "Living well and beautifully and justly are all one thing." We can't seek justice without joy. We can't find the deepest kind of happiness without engaging in a life of service. We can't have only good without any bad. We can't love others without loving ourselves. It's when we balance wellbeing, beauty, and justice within a community that we can flourish.

What Socrates said kind of reminds me of my favourite verse that I read in the Bible as a child: "And what does the Lord require of you? To act justly, to love mercy, and to walk humbly with your God."* It is not one or the other. The choice is not between darkness or light, or between happiness or sorrow. It's all of it. In this life, we will experience beauty and barrenness, bliss and lament, inspiration and disillusionment—sometimes all at once.

I want to thank you, the reader, in advance for buying, reading, or sharing my book. Writing it has been painful and helpful as I dip into the archives of memories I'd rather forget and experiences I still am trying to reconcile. It has been difficult but also a healing and restorative part of my journey.

I wrote this book for me, but also for you. I wrote it for you, the burned out humanitarian in Nigeria silently asking *why me?* I wrote it for you, the disillusioned non-profit staff member in the Midwest wondering if anyone else in the world is feeling what you're feeling. I wrote it for you, the passionate but new kid on the block who's trying to figure out your next steps in seeking justice. If you've ever dreamt of doing your part of good for the world, then I wrote this book for you.

You don't need to agree what I have to say. I caution you that you some of what I do say may make you feel uncomfortable. If you'd rather not be challenged right now, then this book may

---

* Micah 6:8 NIV.

not be for you. What I have to say isn't necessarily "right" or "wrong", but is meant to start a conversation, to cultivate deep thinking, and maybe even encourage you to do things a little differently.

I don't have answers, but I do have experiences and I've shown up to share them with you. My experiences aren't conclusive, but they do help to define what I now know. Some of these stories I'll share with you in this book. I've chosen to be as vulnerable and honest as it is appropriate in this context, so I invite you to come on this introspective journey with gentleness and an open mind.

In case you were wondering, those two wise people I mentioned earlier are my parents. And so it is to them that I dedicate this book. Along with my beautiful sister, Kristy, my family loved me right from the beginning and through my darkest times. Thanks, Mom and Dad, for supporting me as I fall in love again with the vocation I was commissioned to do. I love you.

TERMS

The following are terms I frequently use throughout this book. These terms may be popularly understood differently from how I use them in this particular context. In order to debunk some of the negative connotations and to clarify my own perception of them, below are my own definitions of these key terms:

broken / brokenness: The universal human experience of realizing our finite nature and accepting we aren't perfect. It is neither a flaw nor a source of shame, but can be an empowering and productive experience.

burnout: This is more than tiredness from working a series of long shifts or being stressed from a project at work. In this context, *burnout* is emotional, mental, physical, and spiritual exhaustion to the point of depletion.

humanitarian: Anyone who considers it his or her vocation to live a life of service. It doesn't have to be someone who lives overseas or someone who would consider himself or herself noble. It is someone who wants to do good for others in any part of the world, including their own.

human trafficking: The illegal trade in human beings for the purposes of commercial sexual exploitation or forced labour.

justice: No word in this book is more difficult to define than *justice*. My use of it refers to the whole process of seeking the entire spectrum of love, mercy, service, altruism, ethics, truth, integrity, law, and righteousness, all of which encompass *justice*.[1] I used the terms *justice* and *social justice* interchangeably.

non-governmental organization (NGO): A registered agency operating without governmental council but that may rely on governmental funding. In this context, I mainly refer to NGOs as humanitarian agencies operating internationally.

non-profit: Used synonymously with *social justice organization* in this context. See below.

social justice advocate: Used synonymously with *humanitarian*. See above.

social justice organization: An organization with registered charitable status designed for an express purpose other than financial profit, especially to address a social issue or injustice. Used synonymously with *non-profit* in this context.

survivor: A person who has endured a harrowing and sometimes traumatizing life event, such as abuse or exploitation. Most often, I use this term referencing somebody who has escaped or lived through human trafficking.

---

[1]   Ken Wytsma, Pursuing Justice (Nashville: Thomas Nelson, 2013), 4.

Living well
and beautifully
and justly
are all one thing.
—Socrates

INTRODUCTION

When Justice Is Hollow

Let [she] who would move the world first move [herself].
—Socrates

I have a secret.

Whenever I see my friend Keturah—which isn't all that often, since an international boundary line bisects our friendship—we come parched for a certain kind of conversation about social justice that we can't have anywhere else.

Keturah and I have worked in the sphere of human trafficking interventions for long enough to know there are certain opinions we must keep to ourselves. There are burdens all justice advocates silently bear. We can't publicly admit them, though, out of fear our secret will simultaneously diminish the credibility of our work and the value of our souls. We are too embarrassed, too ashamed, too fearful to speak the truths we conceal. And yet, for Keturah and I, these truths need to be articulated outside of our soul-to-soul coffee dates and international Skype calls, because we don't hear them spoken anywhere else.

With some degree of reluctance, I started bringing my own secret to light a few years ago. I was attending a conference for justice professionals with the hope of returning with more inspirational guidance to my work. At the start of that weekend, I listened to a lecture about seeking justice in a consumer-driven culture—that, ironically enough, was hosted in the Tiffany Ballroom of a luxury hotel, with water served from disposable plastic cups.

I spent most of that weekend a little shocked by the watered-down conference sessions. They were sandwiched between ten-minute, high-entertainment concerts designed for a low-attention-span crowd. By the end of it, I felt compelled to admit something I'd never spoken aloud.

I'm tired of justice.

Don't get me wrong. It's not justice itself that perturbs me; it's how we've come to understand and politicize it.

In my own experiences of humanitarian service from Canada to Cambodia, from Mexico to metropolitan California, it seems we often contort justice to fit our own agendas. We define its dimensions according to our levels of commitment to it. We speak of it to flatter ourselves, inserting "justice issues" casually but strategically into conversations as if it gives us more buoyancy in the human struggle for worthiness. We glamorize what it means to be a humanitarian. We sensationalize justice without unpacking what it really means or looks like.

And I'm tired of it.

I'm tired of justice being talked about without being sought. I'm tired of the monologues spoken from soapboxes, being talked *at* instead of encouraged *by* the self-appointed leaders of the justice movement. I'm tired of watching hands outstretched to God during worship that don't reach out to their neighbours, tired of tears cried from pews for the suffering of the world while hands lie idle in doing anything about it.

I'm tired of all the hype. I'm tired of human trafficking being more of a flashy buzzword than a social and economic crisis. I'm tired of when fair trade is more about what's trendy than what's ethical, responsible, or right.

I'm tired of justice being so diluted that we become deluded. I'm tired of filtering it into easily digestible, bite-sized pieces channelled through some social media outlet to appease our eroding attention spans. I'm tired of 140-character, quotable sound bites serving as the central and sometimes exclusive informant of our educational experience of global inequities.

I'm tired of justice organizations being run unjustly. I'm tired of poverty-alleviation organizations hosting their staff conferences and retreats at five-star resorts and paying their CEOs enough money to travel by private jet. I'm tired of the virtuous façades some non-governmental organizations (NGOs) use to shroud corrupt strategies and poisoned motives. I'm tired of when a mission's prestige and profit are emphasized more than the mission itself.

I'm tired of justice being an outlet for displaying our edited and ideal selves. I'm tired of seeing a good cause being used as a virtuous veneer we hide behind to leverage our moral statuses, distracting others from seeing our flaws, fears, and failures. I'm tired of justice validating our worth, because, deep down, I wonder if our altruistic efforts are sometimes more about how we make *ourselves* look and feel when we build that school, sponsor that child, dig that well.

I'm tired of half-truths and partial stories. I'm tired of hearing about nobility and righteousness without also hearing about the true costs and equally real experiences of doubt, disbelief, and discouragement. I'm tired of not hearing about what a disillusioning experience it can be to work for justice, tired of amplifying stories of success rather than hearing authentic stories of the journey.

I'm tired of how working for justice can make me a doormat. I'm tired of how it blurs the line between volunteering my time and getting paid fairly for it. I'm tired of how justice typically means taking time off isn't seen as a reflection of healthy boundaries but is stamped as a selfish act that calls my dedication into question. It means wearing a badge of honour at all times. It means being rewarded for reckless bravado while trying to build a humanitarian empire without ever pausing to address my own needs.

I'm tired of justice being a thing we do instead of the people we are. I'm tired of it being a job we have, not a lifestyle we live. I'm tired of being so disconnected from seeking justice that we have to use organizations with registered charitable statuses as brokers for our compassion. I'm tired of being comfortable talking about justice in conference halls and boardrooms—especially when it comes to doing justice in somebody else's country—without knowing what to do with homelessness we encounter it on our own streets.

All in all, I'm tired of when justice is hollow. When justice is hollow, it's nothing more than a patch on a backpack, a bracelet on a wrist, or a bumper sticker on a car. When justice is more about promoting the celebrity status of the organization than the survival status of those it serves, it's come to be a guise, a trend, a product. It stops being about justice and is more about "just us."

My friend Keturah and I are ready for a change, and we're not the only ones. She and I have weathered the storms of burnout and disillusionment along our journeys of justice, just like many others. We're only two of countless baffled and bruised seekers of justice who ache for solidarity and desperately hope the truth will humanize rather than vilify us. We think it's time to revolutionize our approaches, to pursue justice greatly but also sustainably, to work audaciously but wisely—not perfectly, not unrealistically, and certainly not on our own.

We're ready to change the conversation about justice.

We're ready to see souls, not victims. We're ready to learn to let go of the saviour complex, the insatiable desire to make a project out of "fixing" people. We're ready to let people speak for themselves, instead of trying to give a voice to someone who already has one.

We're ready to move past talking about justice, even past doing justice, to *being* justice. Good intentions alone do not harness the power of justice. Words of unfettered idealism untied to tangible and realistic action cannot bring meaningful change. We're ready for justice to be not jobs we have but lifestyles we live; not a thing we do but people we are.

But we're also ready to strip those badges of honour we're supposed to carry. Sometimes even the most impassioned convictions, the most rigorously planned strategies, and the longest working hours don't always lead to the outcomes we anticipate. So we're ready to talk about the times our efforts to seek justice implode. We need to speak our struggles instead of distract others from seeing our authentic, messy selves. We need to destroy the illusion of nobility and be humans with needs and emotions, not heroes without boundaries or limits.

We're ready to readjust our expectations of ourselves as humanitarians. It's time we free ourselves from the myth that we possess infinite compassion and interminable zeal to help, hope, serve, and sacrifice. It's time we give ourselves the grace to replenish our souls and respond to our needs without fear of judgment or ostracism.

We're ready to see an end to the consistent inconsistencies of the organizations for which we work. To see anti-trafficking organizations stop trying to break the cycle of poverty and exploitation in communities by guilting their own staff into working seven-day weeks for the sake of the cause. To stop cultivating a culture of perfectionism. To stop breeding a disease of burnout in order to achieve our goal. And to start believing staff care is not only possible but necessary.

We're ready to talk about the triumphs *and* trials. We're ready to fill the gaps left by sensationalized stories and half-truths about the "adventures" and "rewards" of humanitarian work by also mobilizing honest discussions of its darkness and despair. We want to learn how to accept the coexistence of beauty and affliction, of victory and defeat, of joy and pain in the pursuit of justice.

We're ready to address the elephant in the room, too. We're ready to talk candidly and shamelessly about mental health. We're ready to de-stigmatize anxiety, depression, post-traumatic stress, and compassion fatigue. These are only a few of the burdens justice workers increasingly carry but are too ashamed to admit and address. We're ready to stop using suffering as the ultimate goal of justice workers and to start balancing work with rest, and truth with grace.

We're ready to shift the conversation about changing the world toward how to change *ourselves*. Too often we try to solve the problems in other countries because we're ashamed of the injustices permeating our borders. We try to fix the brokenness in other people because it's easier than addressing the brokenness we conceal in ourselves. We're ready to start identifying our need to be rescued and redeemed from our own pain and dysfunctions before trying to rescue and redeem others.

Because the truth is, pursuing justice doesn't always give the personal return on investment we want. Sometimes we're given suffering and scars that don't always make sense—in the moment, or possibly ever. It's especially in those eras of disillusionment that we need to permit the people who re-build our communities to embrace their humanity before heroism. We need justice workers who can serve lovingly, deeply, and empathetically, instead of breeding a generation of dehumanized humanitarians.

Yes, we are tired for a litany of reasons—and tired of being tired. But we are also ready to open the dialogue. We are ready to reclaim and redeem how we see and seek justice. We are ready to do things differently.

And as we do that, we need to start understanding that perhaps we're so tired because justice isn't always something we can achieve, something we bestow upon others, something we can measure. Perhaps it's something we endeavour toward. Perhaps it's something that has no perfect formula or straightforward strategy, something that is only learned through trial and error while sought over time. Perhaps it's something we pursue, however imperfectly, in a culture of community and grace.

Perhaps justice just is.

PART I

LIVING JUSTLY

Few will have the greatness to bend history itself,
but each of us can work to change a small portion of events.
It is from numberless diverse acts of courage and belief
that human history is shaped.
Each time a [person] stands up for an ideal,
or acts to improve the lot of others,
or strikes out against injustice,
he [or she] sends forth a tiny ripple of hope,
crossing each other from a million different centers of energy
and daring those ripples to build a current
which can sweep down the mightiest walls
of oppression and resistance.
—Robert Kennedy

CHAPTER 1

With Passion, Possibility, and Purpose: Reconfigured Dreams

It's a dangerous business, Frodo, going out your door …
You step into the Road, and if you don't
keep your feet, there's no knowing
where you might be swept off to.
—J. R. R. Tolkien, *The Fellowship of the Ring*

Us three kids contrived the plan where most kids come up with all ideas that have height: the trampoline.

"We should call ourselves the Emeralds!" I piped up between jumps.

"No, we should be the *Sparkling* Emeralds!" my nine-year-old sister chimed in with her alluring adjective, only two years my senior but with infinitely more authority when it came to play.

Together with our friend April, we were devising policy and strategy for a new club. The Emeralds—rather, the Sparkling Emeralds—were to become somewhat of a spy network we would use for the express purpose of doing good deeds in our neighbourhood in total secrecy. The Christmas prior, Santa Claus had gifted my sister and I with a pair of new walkie-talkies—the quintessential tool for engaging in any kind of undercover work with excellence. We were equipped and ready to start our undercover neighbourhood clean-up service.

Our plan, however, had a flaw. Not that it didn't work—after all, we spent autumn raking leaves and winter shovelling snow with such gusto that we were running out of lawns in our neighbourhood to tend in secret. And by "we," I mostly mean my sister and April. I was charged with the responsibility of being the "lookout officer"—perhaps a polite way of giving me an alternative task in recognition that at barely seven years old, I was too small and slow to handle a rake or a shovel with top-notch efficiency.

So, as you can guess, the hole in our project was in our espionage. Although we had delegated one personnel for full-time spying (me), our neighbours still always managed to attribute the absence of leaves or cleared walkways to the two Bergman sisters and their loyal friend. Later that same day, our neighbours would come to our house with an appreciative smile and a toonie (that would be a two-dollar coin for those outside of Canada) for each of us, along with a hearty thank you to our parents for raising us so well.

One time, our neighbours from across the street caught us in the act and emerged from their house with three cans of grape soda and a plate of homemade cookies fresh out of the oven. Although we were slightly demoralized that our espionage was failing, we graciously accepted the offerings with fervour and then returned to raking leaves.

Our headquarters was located in the basement of our house, which was the Lutheran church parsonage. My sister, our impassioned leader, had scoped out the layout of our house and selected the walk-in closet of the spare bedroom in the basement to be our office. We pushed all the Halloween costumes and cardboard boxes chock full of birthday party decorations out of the way to create space for three small stools. We adorned the walls with posters of droughts in East Africa and natural disasters in Haiti, constant reminders of a world outside the protective walls of our closet—a world aching in far more pain than the sleepy Prairie town that was our home.

Running our operation out of a closet wasn't exactly effective non-profit management, minus the fact that the space was rent-free. Nor were we drawing from sound international development theory by any means, expect for our fluke democratic use of a rotating executive, where we would alternate roles as president, secretary, and treasurer for our meetings. Aside from that, we had no clue what we were doing. But given that some of us were still mastering the art of tying our shoes and telling time on an analog clock, I suppose it was excusable. After all, what we lacked in skill, we made up for in heart.

On a humid August day, our treasurer of the week brought to our attention the fact that our piggy bank was filling up with toonies. My older sister, the mastermind behind most of our shenanigans, suggested we try to accumulate even more toonies by hosting a carnival in our yard. We decided we could use the profits we raised to buy items for the kids in developing countries who received the shoeboxes full of gifts and toys at Christmas—the same kids we saw every day in the posters on our walls.

I was not raised in a house where anything was done half-heartedly, especially when it came to service. So after hanging hand-drawn signs on community lampposts announcing that a spectacular carnival was coming to town, we prepared for the big event by bringing out all the bells and whistles—literally. We had bells and whistles as part of our background soundtrack.

The three of us dressed up in clown costumes for the carnival. My mom had spent years putting together a Tickle Trunk full of costumes, just like the one we saw on the Canadian television series *Mr. Dressup*. The trunk contained all kinds of memorabilia—including clown suits—bought from garage sales and thrift stores to vitalize the imagination and make-believe play of children like us.

Much to our delight, people actually showed up to our carnival. I'm not entirely convinced that they were enticed by the colourful poster-board signs on the lampposts scattered across town, and I still have my suspicions that my mom called up everyone from our church and coaxed them to come. Regardless, we gave them a show—a *real* show.

We pushed together oversized utility boxes to create a maze for kids to crawl through. My sister and I recruited our mom to sew together scraps of fuchsia *Lion King* fabric, which we filled with stale soybeans for a beanbag toss. We gave out popsicles and lemonade and balloon animals. We strung up a blue camping tarp across two trees so that carnival attendees could "fish" for a prize on the other side with a pole fashioned from a stick and a long strand of yarn. And, because our parents always emphasized the importance of early child development through reading, we obediently set up a reading corner with our mom's old camping tent from her year of backpacking in Europe when she was in her twenties. We piled the tent with pillows and storybooks, and then were bewildered that we were the only kids in attendance who thought a reading corner at a carnival was a cool idea.

No matter what, it was all for fun and all for good.

After our last guest left late that afternoon, we counted up all the toonies and quarters and dimes stored carefully in our makeshift cashbox. Our triumphant discovery was that we had made a grand total of thirty-three dollars in donations. Given that our only frame of reference was the cost of an ice cream cone or a daily pass to the swimming pool, thirty-three dollars was a lot to wrap our elementary school minds around.

Blissfully, we added the carnival fund to our piggy bank containing the entire accumulation of every lemonade stand and donation from our not-so-secret neighbourhood clean-up agency. My parents drove us into the big city forty-five minutes down the road, where we used our funds to purchase items for ten shoeboxes that we shipped off to kids who had never received a Christmas present before. From there, a dream was born.

A Life of Service

My idealistic roots formed while growing up in that quiet, humble town in the heart of the Prairies. Amid the canola fields and old-fashioned grain elevators of the rural farming community, I spent my childhood developing an unquenchable passion for peace and justice.

I was born into an inherently purpose-driven family—the kind of family that would forgo regular gift giving to donate instead to charities, the kind of family that would invite lonely and widowed seniors for Christmas Eve dinner every year. With my mom working as a nurse and my dad as a pastor for over thirty years each, my parents set a quiet example of how to transform the call to serve others into a lifelong vocation.

As a dynamic team of two professional helpers, my parents cultivated an environment of self-discovery to help my older sister and me identify our own strengths and gifts in order to serve others as well. By the time I was eight years old, my zealous parents plunked me down at the kitchen table that I could barely see over, and we worked our way through the Myers-Briggs indicators to assess my personality style. As premature as the activity may have been, it was also prophetic, because my results turned out to be completely congruent with a lifestyle of service.

We thrived, my sister and I, as we grew up in a purpose-driven environment that my parents carefully balanced with love, beauty, and adventure. Our family spent winters tucked away in the snow-capped Rocky Mountains and summers tenting in mossy forests or playing on the beach of our lakeshore cabin. We learned to live well and to live fully in our quest for purpose beyond the tangible.

Yet while my parents did all they could to open my eyes to the beauty of the world, they also did not hide from me the human-made injustices that were polluting it. My parents transmitted messages of justice by introducing me to the stories of Martin Luther King Jr. and other leaders of historic and heroic influence who spent their lives countering evil. It lit a fire within me. Stoked by historical non-fiction, heart-wrenching documentaries, and impassioned dinnertime conversations, my zeal for humanitarian service grew.

Beyond the influences of my family life, the pleasantly dynamic Lutheran church I grew up in was another integral source for teaching me how to use my faith as a channel for activism. From the time I was seven, I worked my way up the ranks of layperson assembly lines to organize and deliver baskets of emergency household supplies for low-income families in our community. I tagged along with my heavily church-involved parents to visit congregation members at the nursing home, watching in admiration as both of my parents would bring laughter and joy to bedridden senior citizens.

I also garnered a deep appreciation for our church's global focus in sponsoring overseas missionaries. Frequently, the missionaries our church supported would stay overnight at my family's house and share profound stories about serving marginalized people in countries I'd never heard of—places like Mozambique and Indonesia and the Cameroon, places that rolled off my tongue with sweet intrigue and spiked my appetite for travel. With the spin of our family's globe, the missionaries would point out to my sister and I where they were working. The more I heard their stories and watched slides from their overseas adventures, the more the thought of ameliorating suffering in some of the most remote areas of the world became compelling to me.

And even though I didn't truly understand what it meant at the time, I decided to dedicate my life to seeking justice.

Katie Bergman

Seeking an Outlet to Seek Justice

Beyond home and church, it was difficult to find an avenue to fully live out my desire for engaging in full-time humanitarian service. My town of 1,200 people was limited in resources, especially to equip young people to become overseas relief workers or even local advocates of justice. Most of my peers were either expected to pursue a sensible post-secondary degree in one of two big cities in Saskatchewan or to take over the family farm immediately after graduation. Humanitarianism wasn't practical enough to be on anyone's radar.

In the public school system, my peers and I were conditioned to pursue careers, not something as metaphysical as a "calling." We took career guidance courses in junior high, made appointments with a career counsellor to take career tests in high school, prepared to submit post-secondary applications for the purpose of gaining a career, and attended every career fair under the sun to have a plan lined up to immediately start generating a disposable income after graduating from university.

The contrast between calling and career started becoming confusing to me as a sixth-grade student when I enrolled in a class that allowed us to explore our professional options after we graduated from high school. Our final project was to choose a job from a list of standard work opportunities and research its educational prerequisites, potential income, and benefits. And as an idealistic twelve-year-old, using such a logical and structured approach to planning my future did not bode well with me.

Alternatively, I compiled lists of more existential "benefits" to the purpose-driven work I aspired to pursue one day. But as it turned out, "building character" or "ending global poverty" were not the kinds of benefits my teacher had in mind. He tried to gently steer me back on track, telling me that benefits, in this context, had more to do with a good health care plan than the joy of caring for the world. I was disappointed, even bored, by the thought of having to present to my class about dental plans and paid sick leave—benefits that would only benefit me and nobody else.

Little options remained for those of us who didn't fit into the cookie-cutter model, so I floundered my way through high school in search of an outlet for social justice service. At minimum, I fulfilled the glorified expectations of a well-behaved pastor's daughter, which meant being actively involved in altruistic efforts in the community. Yet hosting chilli-sale fundraisers or babysitting my teachers' kids or volunteering as a youth mentor still couldn't busy me enough to quell my longing for something a little deeper, something a little more meaningful.

Eventually, I desperately resorted to an attempt at entrepreneurialism. I created my own outlet by trying to launch a social movement in my high school to raise awareness and funds for HIV/AIDS orphans in sub-Saharan Africa. But as a naive seventeen-year-old without the knowledge of running a start-up and having no access to any kind of tangible resources, my aspirations led to little more than a series of wistful conversations and unproductive planning meetings with a handful of half-interested students with nothing better to do on their lunch break.

Public school wasn't the only place lacking in tangible mechanisms to equip me for the social justice world. Most everything around me—from culture, social networking, and the media to educational, economic, and political institutions—seemed to subconsciously or provocatively extol the kind of work that brings personal prosperity and prestige above all else. Public funding gives preference to fields of study in science, technology, engineering, and math. Political leaders repeatedly glorify economy-building work, like President Obama in his State of the Union address in 2011, when he verbally envisioned "an America that attracts a new generation of high-tech manufacturing and high-paying jobs."[1] Seldom have I heard North American political leaders rally their country to pursue humanitarian endeavours.

Given this pressure, universities have to facilitate a direct transition from student life to obtaining a lucrative job. Increasingly, this means dispensing of liberal arts programming and giving preference for subject areas considered to be more suitable in the wake of an economic recession. Sometimes, as a bachelor of arts student, I was scoffed at by fellow university students seeking more "practical" degrees, who often assured me I'd never be able to find a real job.

In those moments, I had to remind myself that some of the world's most heralded thinkers, writers, and activists were people who majored in liberal arts, like bestselling writer J. K. Rowling, who had studied French; Steven Spielberg, who had majored in English; and the founder of CNN, Ted Turner, who had studied classics. There was Nelson Mandela, who had studied anthropology and earned a BA. Or Craig Keilburger, co-founder of Free the Children, who had graduated with a degree in peace and conflict studies. Since few others widely promoted these kinds of obscure areas of study, I had to coach myself to validate my choice to seek justice as my lifelong profession. But, especially as a young and impressionable university student, it wasn't easy.

The hardest part was trying to guard myself from cynicism. It was hard not to feel as if the training that equipped professionals for mending broken homes and communities was grossly undervalued by the rest of society. To me, it seemed that education that focused on cultivating imagination, diversifying intellect, and developing reasoned inquiry was considered impractical. Somehow, the work that, in the words of twentieth-century philosopher Russell Kirk, could "order the soul and order the republic" seemed to be largely regarded as inconsequential. And so, with fewer investments in humanitarian services and less interest of students studying liberal arts and service-related fields, the non-profit industry struggles to gain a 2 percent share of the American GDP per year.[2] In fact, Americans spend more on their military,[3] cosmetics,[4] and pet care products[5] than they do on charitable donations.

Of course, most of us admit that volunteering and altruism may have a role within one's life or career, but it's often something to be done on the side or in one's spare time. It's kind of like ordering the obligatory side salad to appear healthy and balanced to everyone else. And to me, that wasn't enough.

Coming Full Circle

When that empty belief—that a career is about enumeration of personal and professional accomplishments—failed to appeal to me, I had to forge my own path. Through trial and error—but mostly error—one pursuit eventually led to another and then another. High school graduation transitioned into pursuing a degree in human justice. Living in the stillness of the Prairies led to roaming nomadically throughout the globe. And over fifteen years after I mailed my first shoebox to a child in a developing country, I wound up standing under an unforgiving sun in Southeast Asia, distributing shoeboxes packed by the next generation of young, aspiring social justice advocates from all over the world.

Life seemed to come full circle. Except that where I'd ended up wasn't exactly what I'd expected.

After a two-hour bumpy bus ride, my team and I arrived at a remote village in rural Cambodia and began hauling out dozens of crates filled with gifts. We played games with an elated crowd of well-behaved boys and girls under ten years old who sat on a spread of woven mats with exerted patience as they waited for the contents of those huge crates containing their gifts to be opened.

Our leader spoke in Khmer about how much God loves them and how each of them is uniquely special. After a brief explanation of where these gifts came from, we began handing out boxes, matching the age and gender specified on the label to each child. Sitting cross-legged, they bounced animatedly until the count of "One, two, two and a half, *three!*" when they tore into their boxes and squealed in delight as they compared their contents with those of their neighbours.

I'll never forget the shy but elated smiles on their faces as they quickly closed their shoeboxes and dispersed, taking off full speed down the dirt road and up the ladders to their houses built on stilts, showing off their new treasures to their parents.

As our group loaded up our overheating bus, we passed by one little barefoot girl in a pink shirt, whose hands pressed together at her nose in a deep bow to show us her silent gratitude. It was only a shoebox, filled with pencils and small toys that someone had bought at a dollar store—but to her, it was precious. I still remember her dancing brown eyes and how her chest swelled as if she were too excited to exhale. She was probably about seven years old—the same age I was when I first started assembling these shoeboxes sent to children in developing countries. I never expected I'd ever meet these children personally one day.

With a trail of cheering children chasing after us, the bus slowly bumped and tousled its way down the dirt road. I tried my best to mimic the euphoric atmosphere bred by my teammates, but something didn't feel right. Here I was serving in Cambodia, where my dreams of pursuing justice came full circle—and I felt nothing. Nothing but drained. And doubtful. And depressed.

During the entire afternoon of frenzied shoebox distribution, I'd defaulted to tuning out the cheering and excitement and caught myself staring directly into the eyes of some of the parents. How did *they* feel about us being here?

Did they feel undermined by these comparatively wealthy, jovial foreigners? Did they fear their children would come to rely on the smiling white faces of Westerners filing from oversized white buses to give imposed handouts, instead of depending on their parents? Did they feel we were trivializing their problems by bringing in shoeboxes full of stuffed animals and hard candy when none of their children had shoes or even breakfast that morning? Did they think we didn't care that their well had run dry, that their crops weren't producing, or that they couldn't find jobs because they didn't know how to read? Was our trip to their village nothing but unsolicited charity?

My gaze then had fallen on the children—children who had to grow up far too fast. Children who spent their days working in factories to bring home a few extra pennies for their families …

And that's when it dawned on me. These cheap toys, the ones that Westerners had bought at a dollar store and shipped overseas—could they have wound back into the tiny hands that had originally made them in the first place?

Certainly, there were moments from that sweltering day out in the rural Cambodian village that I treasured—like the four tiny boys sitting cross-legged neatly in a row as they ripped into their shoeboxes, only to quickly close them because of the Cambodian belief that it's rude to open a gift in front of somebody, or that little girl in a pink shirt who thanked us in a respectful bow.

Yet these fond images became shrouded by the guilt I felt as I rode the bus back to the hotel with the rest of the team. Were our games and songs and gifts enough? Did we actually impact the community the way we would be reporting back to our churches? Were we more harmful than helpful?

A New Dream

As it turned out, working for justice hadn't culminated into the feel-good experience I'd thought it would be. It wasn't saving a different part of the world every day, as I'd dreamt about as a whimsical seven-year-old. It wasn't all valiant acts of service, interspersed with feelings of accomplishment, as I'd imagined it would be in university. It turned out to be hard—really hard. And confusing. And a lot more complicated than I ever thought possible.

To me, there were three main problems. First, I saw a problem with the way many of us view humanitarianism. A few years into my work, I could see how one-sided the public discourse was and how huge of a discrepancy existed between how other people perceived my work versus the real experience of it. Many people I came across glamorized seeking justice and sensationalized the outcomes. What they didn't know was the tremendous disillusionment that comes with it. My acquaintances thought that, as a humanitarian, I went home every night with gratification and the gleaming feeling of a job well done, when, most days, I would go home to a tall glass of wine and the stress of knowing my job is never done. They thought I was out saving souls, when all I was doing was the best I could while my thoughts were becoming jaded, my spirit was waning, and my own soul was fading.

Secondly, I saw a problem with the way we do humanitarianism. Often, we do it without relationship and mutuality. We turn people into projects, trying to speak for them and save them, which often means objectifying, paternalizing, and even re-victimizing them. I've seen too many agencies try help in the name of justice, only to create greater disunity and damage.

And thirdly, I saw a problem with the way we tend to be humanitarians. We lead with the assumption that we'll be able to save everyone in our path. We have such high expectations of what it means to work for justice that we face-plant into bitterness and disillusionment, compassion fatigue and burnout. We take the *human* out of humanitarianism.

All of this combined was a tough discovery. After all, I'd grown up with the idealized notion that being a humanitarian was exclusively a rewarding and noble enterprise, because nobody told me differently. The paper pushing, the late nights of proposal writing, the struggles and internal politics of non-profit organizations, the sickening feelings of watching gruesome things happening to the ones we're caring for, the despair of watching darkness take over … I hadn't expected any of it.

After only a few years of humanitarian service, I was fed up. It was an endless battle against outrageous expectations and serial perfectionism. It was a constant struggle of balance, asking myself tough questions to which I had no answers. Questions like: *How do I have enough compassion to identify and empathize with the pain of another person without taking responsibility for them? How do I extend humanity and even love to a John or trafficker without condoning what they do? How do I manage my emotional impulses to avoid being a heavy-handed helper when all I want to do is fix and rescue and save?*

I was tired of justice: tired *from* being tired and tired *of* being tired. But it wasn't that I simply needed a break from it. I took plenty of those—from a two-month solo backpacking excursion in Eastern Europe to a half-year sabbatical at a home tucked away in the woods in Canada. It was more about needing my entire system to reboot. I was so depleted that I felt I had nothing left to give. I felt nothing at all.

At my lowest point along the trajectory of my journey, I needed something new. It wasn't that I needed a new cause or a new vocation or a new country to live in. I needed a new way of looking at justice. And in my efforts to be a little kinder to the world, I also needed to learn to be a little kinder to myself.

My dreams are not the same anymore. I'm not the same anymore. And now that I've seen some of it, the world is not the same conquerable sphere it once was to me as a child. The ideals I had as a seven-year-old would-be world changer have been put through fire, shattered by hopelessness, and then strengthened against resistance that still, to this day, continues to push the limits of my pursuit.

I've acquired a new form of idealism. It's not the glamorized notion of humanitarian work featured in non-profit newsletters and websites, nor is it the limited perspective I had as a student of justice. It's imperfect, but it's real—it's mine. It sees both the good and the bad about handing out toys to kids in rural villages of developing countries. It acknowledges the simplicity of compassion and the complexities of justice in a world that holds the capacity for both love and hatred. It accepts the need for hope-filled service and the reality of human limitations. And even today, it's learning when to hold on and when to let go.

Some days—many days, in fact—I'm not always sure why I'm still fighting for justice when it's left me so broken. When I'm counselling a traumatized staff or swimming in a sea of paperwork, I don't feel as if my work is noble or even terribly rewarding—because there is no reward in watching people suffer. There are times I question whether or not it's worth it. Most days, it just feels hard—really, really hard.

Why do I seek justice, especially when it is unfathomably difficult and unequivocally disillusioning? Because even though I don't have all the answers, I do have experiences—and each one of them has taught me that it's not only possible to keep fighting in a broken system where nothing is perfect, but it's also necessary. Because my heart is tethered, my idealism has been tempered, and my soul is tenaciously drawn to the hopeful belief that if we created an unjust world, then we can change it.

We have to.

---

[1] Barack Obama, "Remarks by the President in the State of the Union Address," White House, January 24, 2012, http://www.whitehouse.gov/the-press-office/2012/01/24/remarks-president-state-union-address.

[2] Suzanne Perry, "The Stubborn 2% Giving Rate," Chronicle of Philanthropy, June 17, 2013, http://philanthropy.com/article/The-Stubborn-2-Giving-Rate/139811/.

[3] Dinah Walker, "Trends in U.S. Military Spending," Council on Foreign Relations, July 15, 2014, http://www.cfr.org/defense-budget/trends-us-military-spending/p28855.

[4] Annamaria Andriotis, "10 Things the Beauty Industry Won't Tell You," Market Watch, April 20, 2011, http://www.marketwatch.com/story/10-things-the-beauty-industry-wont-tell-you-1303249279432.

[5] Derek Thomas, "These 4 Charts Explain Exactly How Americans Spend $52 Billion on Our Pets in a Year," Atlantic, February 13, 2013, http://www.theatlantic.com/business/archive/2013/02/these-4-charts-explain-exactly-how-americans-spend-52-billion-on-our-pets-in-a-year/273446/.

CHAPTER 2

Growing Pains:
Discovering Disillusionment

A lie that is half-truth is the darkest of all lies.
—Alfred Tennyson

The windshield of our car was dotted with droplets of moisture, blown by heavy winds from the apex of the waterfall. As my friend slowly steered the car through the park entrance, we started to hear the thunderous roar of the cascades we'd travelled so far to see.

The summer I graduated from university, my best friend, Sarah, and I spent a month camping our way through Eastern Canada. We scoped out Toronto from the top of the CN Tower, climbed the rocky shoreline of Peggy's Cove outside of Halifax, and tented on the coastal mountains of the Cabot Trail in Nova Scotia's Cape Breton Island. We ordered *crêpes au français* in Québec, splashed in the Bay of Fundy at low tide, and sprawled out on the sandy beaches of Prince Edward Island. Within the seven thousand kilometres we travelled, we even managed to take a ferry across to the easternmost point in Canada vis-à-vis St. John's, Newfoundland.

Our month of travels culminated in the grandiose moment of seeing Niagara Falls. Up until that point, I only had second-hand stories and photoshopped images to inform my perception of its beauty. All my knowledge before that summer was borrowed or dreamt up, leaving ample space for my imagination to carve out elaborate details of what it was like to see the falls for myself.

Years of creative fantasizing built up to that moment I imagined would be nothing short of magical. What I anticipated was a tastefully preserved natural paradise, burgeoning in its breathtaking majesty. And yet, as our car crept through a series of nondescript cement parking lots, I came to the surprising discovery that we had arrived to a mini Las Vegas.

Dejectedly, I pushed through crowds of foreign tourists adorned in wide-brimmed Tilley hats and fanny packs on a quest to find that taste of nature I came for. Niagara Falls, while beautiful and still retaining its authentic flavour, had become overpowered by the artificial pungency of mini Vegas in all its flashy neon splendour. It was as if the human species had become envious of the six million cubic feet of water naturally falling over the crest line each minute and tried to outdo it by building a twenty-first century tribute to the Israelites' golden calf in the form of a casino strip and an amusement park. Come for the falls; stay for the artificial fun. Drive thousands of kilometres to explore our tacky settlement of noisy slot machines and arcade games, congested carnival rides and over-stimulating themed restaurants. Marvel at this modern-day Tower of Babel.

With the two extremes of natural beauty and manufactured entertainment competing against each other, it seemed as if Mother Nature was losing the battle. And I was dismayed.

Seven thousand kilometres of travel and years of dreaming about this moment seemed wasted.

Fortunately, disappointment of this kind fades. As our summertime road trip ended and reality returned, I gradually forgot about that anticlimactic experience of seeing Niagara Falls for the first time. That autumn, I dove headfirst into full-time social justice work with grandiose visions for how I would change the world. With high expectations and a low tolerance for disappointment, I began travelling and working abroad with glorified international non-profit organizations that were tackling some of the most egregious global inequities.

As it turns out, my foray into the social justice world ended up being much like showing up to Niagara Falls, ensuing disappointment and all. I wanted to be part of something authentic, something beautiful, something meaningful. Instead, I discovered a very different world: a world with compromised integrity, overrun by artificial props to mask the unsavoury realities of human nature.

Just like Niagara Falls, I did find elements of beauty and traces of authenticity in the humanitarian sector. But I also found many other things I hadn't bargained for. Yes, I found justice and mercy and grace—yet not always in the same magnitude as I found superficial distractions and empty gestures of self-fulfillment masquerading as charity.

Disappointment is inevitable whenever hope and expectations and unbridled aspirations exist in tangled unison. For myself, where I expected to find honour, I found corruption. Where I came to see restorative work, I found malignancy. In the place I sought out clarity and purpose, I found disillusionment—which, surprisingly, turned out to be one of the greatest things that could happen to me.

Discovering Disappointment

As a rookie humanitarian, I was destined to have that first harsh experience of battered expectations in the social justice sphere sooner or later. And at age twenty-one, I found mine in a paradoxical place—a place that superimposed my most gratifying experience of service with my most embittering one: in a swarm of dust and children in the desert of rural Mexico.

It was a jolting introduction to the life of a humanitarian. I was assigned to teach a group of children with special needs, most of whom lived in decrepit, one-room housing and came to school without food in their bellies. My favourite student lived with her parents and younger brother in a house the size of my bathroom back in Canada, built with sticks and garbage bags that wrapped around the house as makeshift walls that couldn't quite keep the rain out.

It was close to the end of my time in Mexico when my favourite student suddenly disappeared. She wasn't waiting with her mom and little brother for the school bus to pick her up at the end of the dirt road one October morning … or the next morning, or the next after that. Our staff searched for her, but it was clear her parents were gone without a trace, and her neighbours had no information on their whereabouts.

To me, that just meant we had to look a little harder. To my supervisors, that meant the case was closed.

Being new to the field, I wasn't sure which was more shocking: the disappearance of a student or the complacency of the organization. I thought we were supposed to be missionary MacGyvers: skilful problem solvers, non-violent protectors of the good, unrelenting ambassadors of restoring rightness to wrong situations. Didn't my supervisors realize that this student could have been kidnapped by traffickers and sold into forced labour? Couldn't they see we should be filling in the gaps that a corrupt and apathetic government was ignoring?

Yet every time I asked one of my supervisors what kind of measures we were going to take to find this student, I was met with the same vacant answer: "We've done all we can, Katie."

Whether it was naïveté or inexperience or perfectionism, I couldn't accept that answer. To me, "doing all we can" implied that every avenue of search and rescue had been considered and explored. It meant temporarily suspending our own convenience and comfort until no other options remained but to finally withdraw.

Paralyzed by discouragement, I started wondering if there were other humanitarians out there struggling to work for an organization that seemed to do just enough to appease our donors and maintain saintly appearances. Were there others out there like me feeling secretly disenchanted?

All fears that my student was forever lost to exploitative circumstances were dispelled by default when she finally showed up to school again after an agonizing month without answers. Even though she was back in safe hands, her return wasn't an exchange for my deep disappointment in the way my organization had handled the frightening disappearance.

It wasn't the last time I felt let down by a non-profit I trusted. At the outset of my journey, I thought I had entered into a world of big-hearted people with pure motives and a unified drive for a common cause of global redemption. After only a couple of years, I thought I had mistakenly entered some vortex of tragic discontinuity, where half-hearted attempts at resettling refugees or rehabilitating child soldiers seemed to be less about justice and more about self-gratification.

The more time I spent working for justice, the more I became anaesthetized with heavy doses of discouragement. While living in Southeast Asia, I learned of several foreign-run orphanages that had been shut down because their service provision was a guise for embezzlement and corruption. Orphanage owners, often expatriates from wealthy countries, had started launching orphanages as a lucrative business model and profited off of the plight of orphans through foreign donations that were intended to support the children's nutrition, hygiene, and education.[1] On a semi-regular basis, orphanages and other child-protection NGOs made appalling headlines of committing abuse and extortion in the *Phnom Penh Post* and other newspapers.

It wasn't only small-scale organizations hungry for funding that exploited people in the process; even some of the most venerated international organizations had charismatic leaders using deceitful tactics and guilt-inducing appeals to gain global credibility and followership. One of the most globally renowned anti-trafficking NGOs made news in the *Cambodia Daily* in the fall of 2013—not because of winsome efforts to bring healing to the lives of women who had been trafficked but because of fraud.

The ambassador of this Cambodian-based NGO had published a book with her graphic story of being sold into sexual slavery and eventually escaping her exploitative circumstances to launch an aftercare program for fellow trafficking survivors. As it turned out, she had falsified the true accounts of her clients' lives—possibly as a means to gain fame and fortune from sensationalizing their stories.[2] Several clients spoke out and expressed feelings of greater disempowerment and re-victimization by having their fragile personal stories embellished as a desperate means to amplify the organization's status and increase their donor base.

When I first arrived to the social justice field, I naturally expected to see injustice out there in the world—that was why I'd come to help. What I wasn't prepared for was finding injustice so deeply manifested within the internal operations of humanitarian organizations themselves. And before long, I was numb—totally and completely numb.

Redeeming Disappointment

When you grow up with vision obscured by rose-coloured glasses, it's hard to handle disappointment when the glasses finally come off.

Raised as the youngest daughter of a Lutheran pastor's family in a small farming community in the Prairies, I was shielded from many of the disappointing realities of the world and distorted truths presented by popular media. I grew up with books instead of a TV, so I wasn't exposed to the same violent or raunchy shows that were slowly desensitizing my peer group. I retained my wide-eyed innocence and unfettered optimism over the course of my upbringing, convincing myself by the age of seven that I could save the world. I hadn't considered any bridling obstacles—like burnout from believing I could single-handedly save the world, for example.

From the lens of a small-town girl with sanguine expectations and fervent dreams, my beliefs echoed the theories of Rousseau: that people and the world are basically good. Once I left home and began pursuing justice, however, I stepped into a world that was completely antithetical—a world that Thomas Hobbes would gleefully describe as "solitary, poor, nasty, brutish, and short."

This world accepted deceit and betrayal, vindictiveness and self-aggrandizement, hypocrisy and fraudulence. It was a place where domestic abuse and family breakdown, excessive living, and ethical shortcuts were simply considered parts of the "real world." It justified corruption and enslaving innocent people to meet greedy desires. It created a hierarchy of human worth based on criteria like race and sexuality and religion. It perpetuated armed international conflict for political gain and normalized ethnic wars, poverty, and child hunger as unavoidable facts of life.

But of all the disappointing realities I discovered, the worst part of it was how the humanitarian organizations I'd always respected for battling against these problems weren't measuring up to the expectations I had for their zealous pursuit of justice.

It's natural for discouragement to numb us when those we respect choose hatred or power or evil over love. When political leaders live double lives or when venerated athletes use performance-enhancing drugs to get ahead in their career. When co-founders of child-protection organizations are arrested for indecent behaviour. When teachers, pastors, law enforcement personnel, and other respected professionals are convicted for child pornography.[3]

Popular media obsesses over these kinds of gut-wrenching pieces of news. But it is not the whole story. Within each dejecting experience comes an opportunity to redeem the harm that was done. Being disillusioned by the world is not a character flaw. It is not a cataclysmic disaster. Disillusionment is a good thing—if we let it be—because it liberates us with the truth.

Social crusaders throughout history have always played a vital part in transforming disillusioning situations into productive enterprises. There's Upton Sinclair, the muckraking journalist and author of *The Jungle*, whose book served as an infamous exposé of the abhorrent working conditions for recent immigrants in the US meat-packing industry at the turn of the twentieth century. His book caused such a public uproar that it led to the implementation of better worker rights, regulation, and fairer legislation.[4] From his shocking discovery came transformation.

There's Margaret Humphreys, a British social worker in the 1980s, who helped to publicly divulge Britain's sustained use of forcible child migration as a form of child-care policy. It would've been easier for her to be defeated by the shock and disgust that her own government forcibly deported children in state custody to other Commonwealth nations, where some ended up used for cheap manual labour or executed if deemed to be "unfit" based on racial prejudices—all because it was "cheaper" to have other countries caring for them than Britain. Instead of turning a blind eye, she committed her life to exposing the government's use of forced relocation for decades and reconnected thousands of child migrants to their families.[5] She, too, made good use of her dismay.

Or Lois Jenson, a single mother struggling to earn an income in a male-dominated iron-processing plant in the 1970s, who initiated the first class-action sexual harassment lawsuit in the United States. Despite sexual harassment, verbal abuse, intimidation, and stalking from male co-workers used as threats to drop the case, Jenson refused to be silenced and won a major victory for women's rights.[6] She defied her discouragement instead of her discouragement defeating her.

Personally, I've never transformed ethics in the workplace for minorities or influenced the national legal system or redefined human rights on a global scale. But I do know the stifling feeling of being so discouraged that there are only one of two options I can take: fight or flight. Maybe I can also view the disillusionment I've felt not as signs of hopelessness but as reasons to respond. Perhaps I've needed those seasons of deep disappointment to become reconciled with the ugliness in the world, because from this reconciliation comes a renewed passion to do something about it.

Never do I want seeking justice to become just another job. Never do I want to lose that jarring collision of anger meeting grief when I hear the story of a human trafficking survivor or learn about child exploitation happening in my own country. That feeling of disappointment tells me I'm still fighting this fight from a place of compassion. That state of discouragement reminds me that this work is important enough to keep going.

Within disillusionment comes an opportunity: to turn from the clutches of deceit and the crucible of despair and to turn toward the freedom of truth. To transform even the most crushing discoveries into the liberation of ourselves and the enrichment of others.

The Good from the Bad

The life of a humanitarian comes with a series of jarring ramifications. In my own journey, I have felt deep disillusionment from unmet expectations of my own agency, from disappointing decisions made by those I most respected in the social justice sphere. It has deflated my energy, diminished my spirit, and even broken my heart. And yet I've needed to feel that grief in order to move along the continuum from despair to disillusionment to action.

Maybe what we need to survive is forgiveness, the ability to extend grace to the people and organizations who disappoint us—forgiving ourselves when we don't quite measure up to the standard we had for ourselves and forgiving the world for not meeting our expectations.

Maybe the decay of disappointment leaves fertile ground for us to plant a new beginning. Maybe the same experience of discouragement can be used for good.

No, it's not okay for humanitarians or the organizations they work for to resort to corruption. It's not okay to re-victimize survivors of human trafficking by fabricating their stories to gain more followers or to prey off of the vulnerability of orphans for profit. But maybe it's also not okay to demand absolute perfection from humanitarian organizations, as if they are exempt from making the same mistakes we all do.

Naturally, non-profit organizations are accountable to their own actions, as it is with everyone. Part of the problem, though, is that non-profits simply receive a level of criticism that doesn't seem to apply to the rest of the world. Humanitarians are expected to live up to a litany of perfectionistic criteria pruned by someone else's preferences and ideals, and yet it is a standard placed on few other industries. In a way, it's a world set up for failure, because no single organization can fix the world's sorrow and injustices. No individual person could possibly fulfill the expectation of having indestructible ambitions, unbreakable spirits, and an unlimited capacity to love, to serve, and to sacrifice.

After all, it's not a more righteous breed of human being that qualifies for work at Habitat for Humanity or the Red Cross. Some of the most morally upright people may work in the corporate world, and some of the most dispassionate narcissists might have tenure with a non-profit organization. In every field of work, there is both graciousness and greed. There are cases of compassion and corruption. There is a coexistence of integrity and immorality.

Maybe it's time to deconstruct the unrealistic standard humanitarians are expected to meet. Maybe we need to remove that crown of moral superiority from Peace Corps volunteers and overseas missionaries and in-the-trenches advocates to allow them the space to make mistakes in order to grow. Maybe we need to allow humans to be humans, regardless of their kind of vocation.

Teaching kids with special needs in Mexico was one of the first piercing encounters I had with chronic discouragement, and it wouldn't be the last. But it was a critical, coming-of-age moment in my journey. It was the first time I realized how much easier it was to blame my organization for how deeply disappointed I felt about a traumatic ordeal that perhaps was nobody's fault. It was the first twinge of growing pains I'd felt from being part of a world that wasn't as I'd dreamt it to be: a world not ruled by superheroes but governed instead by the same laws and conditions of human boundaries that restricted all mortals.

I've had to come to terms with the gap between the level of control I *think* I have and how much control I *actually* have. And that's easy to resent. There is nothing more demoralizing than pouring time and energy, heart and soul, into trying to help a person who is beyond my reach. It's crushing to be one person trying to combat such a complex and systemic breach of human rights as human trafficking when it never seems to get any better. It's frustrating to dish up meals at soup kitchens or hand out blankets at shelters, wondering if all I'm doing is putting a Band-Aid on a much larger problem.

But maybe there really *is* a point when *we've done all we can* after all.

Even though I was convinced that my willingness to go to infinite lengths to search for my missing student was the hallmark of humanitarian dedication, I had to accept that my own advocacy was flanked by limitations. However reluctant I was, I gradually needed to accept that my sanity hinged on the realization that even humanitarians can't play God. Doing so amplified my need to turn to a higher power, with faith as my foundation and hope as my help.

When years of disappointing discoveries about justice work and my own limitations culminated in deep-seated disillusionment, it was a fusion of paralysis and liberation. As hard as it was to see the world for what it was, it meant I could be freed from the demands of perfection of both others and myself.

Now the question I'd always asked could finally shift from "Why aren't they doing more?" to "At what point do I accept other people's humanity—and mine too?"

[1] Katie Hunt, "Cambodia Shuts Australian-Run Orphanage over Abuse Allegations," CNN, March 26, 2013, http://www.cnn.com/2013/03/26/world/asia/cambodia-orphanage/.

[2] 8 Simon Marks, "Somaly Mam: The Holy Saint (and Sinner) of Sex Trafficking" Newsweek, May 21, 2014, http://www.newsweek.com/2014/05/30/somaly-mam-holy-saint-and-sinner-sex-trafficking-251642.html.

[3] 9 Andrew Palamarchuk, "Toronto Police's Project Spade Results in International Porn Arrests," Inside Toronto, November 14, 2013, http://www.insidetoronto.com/news-story/4219011-toronto-police-s-project-spade-results-in-international-child-porn-arrests/.

[4] 10 Daniel Mark Fogel, "Upton Sinclair," The American Novel, March 2007 http://www.pbs.org/wnet/americannovel/timeline/sinclair.html.

[5] 11 Veronica Lee, "Britain's Child Migrants," Guardian, April 2, 2011, http://www.theguardian.com/lifeandstyle/2011/apr/02/britain-child-migrants-australia-commonwealth.

[6] 12 Suzanne Goldenberg, "It Was like They'd Never Seen a Woman Before," Guardian, February 3, 2006, http://www.theguardian.com/film/2006/feb/03/gender.world.

CHAPTER 3

When Justice Is a Vending Machine: Measuring Impact

Not everything that can be counted counts,
And not everything that counts can be counted.
—William Bruce Cameron

He was homeless and unemployed, born into an unforgivingly hostile environment. I was a university-educated woman who had nearly obtained a double major in justice studies and political science. And yet, despite our different circumstances, he spoke more articulately about politics than I could.

It was one of the first hot days at the start of summer in Winnipeg—the kind of day that pulled everybody outdoors to wander the riverbanks of the Forks or to be lured in by unexpected music and theatre festivals in the streets. My friend Hilary and I were strolling around the rougher edge of the Exchange District in downtown Winnipeg and ended up chatting with three friendly homeless men at a bus stop. They invited us to accompany them to a free community barbecue hosted by a collaboration of church groups. With the three of them as our guides, Hilary and I joined the lineup of passersby with paper plates in hand for our quota of one hot dog and bag of chips per person while listening to them share their stories.

One of them, a tall and lanky man with a bedraggled beard crawling down to his chest, spoke matter-of-factly about how he'd ended up on the streets. Between puffs of a cigarette, he laughed at popular Western diet trends, saying he knew what organic food *really* tasted like, having hunted for sustenance while living off the land for most of his life. He proceeded to lament about Canada being doomed to fail with the current political party in power and how he wouldn't have to resort to such measures for survival if he lived in a more progressive state like Sweden. He spoke as if he had come to terms with life on the streets while also acknowledging the injustice of it.

As a justice professional, I had interacted with plenty of people who were homeless. But what broke my heart the most was hearing how much he felt that social programming—like this church-group organization hosting the barbecue—was failing people like him. Smart people, kind-hearted people, hard-working people who needed more than a freebie—they needed justice.

With a good-natured yet cynical edge, the man gestured toward one of the church volunteers donning a crisp, collared shirt and cream-coloured pants and chuckled, "They give us hot dogs in the name of Jesus."

Justice Oversimplified

The more time I've spent living in and serving a community, the more I've learned how sustainably investing my time, heart, and resources beats giving handouts.

Yet as much as justice is anything but an input-output machine, it's easier and more convenient to oversimplify the work that goes into it. Non-profits struggle to pitch a compelling case for making long-term investments to government funders and high-end individual donors who often prefer short-term funding or supporting projects that produce immediate outcomes.

As a manager of human trafficking prevention programs in Cambodia, I found this most frustrating while facilitating trips for donor teams who came from Western countries to visit and potentially fund our work. On one such occasion, I was assigned to a high-profile team representing some of the most powerful businesses and churches in Canada. In other words, they had a lot of money, and we had our fingers crossed that they'd be willing to give our project some of it.

Hearing the team was from Alberta, I was looking forward to meeting fellow Prairie folk. I expected them to show up with that jovial Canadian accent I missed hearing while being adorned in well-worn jeans and Calgary Flames jerseys. I figured that upon them learning I was from Saskatchewan, they would joke about how the Stampeders were going to crush the Roughriders next football season and then grumble in solidarity about our mutual disdain towards the Eastern Canadian teams in the CFL.

My boss and I met the team in Phnom Penh at the fanciest restaurant I had ever been to in Cambodia. It was a lavish Thai-Khmer restaurant that catered to wealthy tourists who wanted to indulge in local cuisine without having to be drenched in sweat in the dusty streets at an open-air restaurant—which, ironically, would actually constitute an authentic experience.

Hailing from the land of humble farmers, Tim Hortons–toting truckers, and neighbourly backwoods country bumpkins, I was thrown off when the team filed into the private conference room donning neatly pressed suit pants and collared dress shirts. Immediately, I became shamefully aware of two gaping holes in my right pant leg I'd never noticed before. I started feeling gradually uncomfortable with the cavalier remarks of how strongly the food smelled and the hesitant whispers of "Do we really have to sit on the ground to eat?"

Forcing a smile, I tried to bypass the disappointment of not instantly becoming best buddies with my fellow Canadians over a tribute to Stompin' Tom Connors' by singing a boisterous rendition of "The Hockey Song" or an impassioned conversation about how delicious poutine is and reluctantly stuck to business instead. Over the next hour, my boss and I showcased our commitment to holistically preventing human trafficking through a long-term, multi-faceted livelihood development approach. We presented under-reported but profound statistics of how men are nearly twice as likely to be trafficked in certain parts of Cambodia as women, clearly articulating the need for cutting-edge, evidence-based research to serve the range of people vulnerable to exploitation. We showed how we were improving education systems and creating viable economic options to strengthen livelihoods as a preventative measure of human trafficking and other forms of labour exploitation.

Our country director nodded approvingly in constant staccato like a bald bobble head as the two of us passionately discussed our impact and the need to partner with funders like them to continue this work. Yet aside from the pot-bellied team leader snoring from a food coma in the back corner, the only sound

I could hear from the group was the unanimous *zoom!* of our presentation going right over their heads.

The thought of preventing human trafficking by cutting it off at its source was neither glamorous nor immediately satisfying enough for our donors. Instead, the team asked if we could go to the red-light district of Phnom Penh and rescue young women forced into prostitution as the more appealing alternative.

Desperately, we spent the following week on field trips to several remote villages, showing this well-moneyed team of donors that their funding would be designated for effective services addressing the root causes of exploitation. Even through our organization was the vanguard of human trafficking prevention programming in that region of Cambodia, the team was still trying to convince *us* by the end of the week that all we needed to do to stamp out human trafficking was to unshackle women from the brothels and build shelters for them.

Before the team reached their first-class seats on their plane homeward bound for Canada, something became clear to me: Charity was much more enticing to this group than justice. Rather than committing wholeheartedly to a long-term investment based on sound research, they harboured a preference for quick fixes, one-stop-shop solutions, and occasional ten-day mission trips much like this one. And truthfully, I could understand why.

Charity is easy. It's manageable. It makes us feel as if we can throw a dollar at justice without having to sacrifice anything more than what we're willing to give. Most of all, it demands a lot less ownership to address the problems of a far-off country than confronting the systemic inequities built into the foundation of our own homeland.

At the end of the week, as the team loaded up their Louis Vuitton handbags and designer suitcases into their fifteen-passenger van en route to the airport, the silent benediction running through my mind was a quote from St. Augustine: "Charity is no substitute for justice withheld."

Shallow Support, Hollow Justice

"I don't understand how our staff are still so unhappy," complained my exasperated boss while the two of us cleaned up the conference room after a staff meeting. Cringing, I asked him why he felt that way, crossing my fingers I wouldn't get dragged into helping with a human resources overhaul of the non-profit organization he and I worked for. I was already balancing multiple jobs within our non-profit yet being paid for one.

With a genuinely perplexed shake of his head, my boss lamented, "I've done so much for this staff. I've hosted barbecues and beach days for them, sometimes several times in one year. How can they still say I'm unsupportive?"

How? Because sometimes the difference between giving *stuff* and giving support is too much work.

In the justice sphere, the ethics of operating a non-profit organization shouldn't limited to the *what* of the final product in a community alone. It also needs to focus on *how* the work was done—especially if the guiding belief is that a just outcome is born of a just process. That process should consider ethical internal dynamics and practices, which always includes the treatment of staff and volunteers, clients and partners along the way.

Like many other non-profit executive directors, my boss worked hard to meaningfully influence the lives of people in the community we worked in, but he struggled to do the same for his employees. Given the tension between the two approaches to staff care—either lavishing workers with trivial rewards or providing appropriate, genuine, day-to-day support—he often chose the former option. The quicker, easier, less complicated option. The vending-machine option. After all, when so much material, financial, and human capital goes into serving a community, it seems too tedious to funnel energy into staff care too.

There's a problem with that black-and-white option of either offering stuff or support. Trying to compensate for overworking a team by offering staff beach days and barbeques instead of examining the source of the problem from a bottom-up approach never works for long. For those of us at the bottom of the pyramid, we aren't so much in need of stuff. We need support. We need both practical help and mentorship on a consistent basis. We'd like to know that our work is appreciated, that our sacrifices are worth it, that we even matter—not just as cogs in a machine but as humans.

The people we serve don't just want stuff either. They don't want a group of well-meaning tourists disguised as humanitarians to enter their village on a one-time basis and dig them a well when what the village really needs is ongoing job training skills and start-up capital to build a sustainable economic climate. Ribbon-cutting ceremonies unveiling impressive brick schools built by the hands of foreigners may not be as valuable as educational support and resources that makes sense in their context, not an imposition from a Western worldview.

Giving stuff is easy. Creating a change is hard. The first provides more of an instant gratification—the second requires years of developing relationships and shifting attitudes and behaviours while collaboratively influencing long-term, transformative change.

Whether it's help for an entire community or help for a caregiver, the best kind comes in the form of a relationship, not a handout. When support comes with fanfare in nothing more than shiny packages, then the contents of package is empty. When justice is hollow, it isn't justice at all.

Measuring Justice

When it comes to justice, we want an outcome that we can measure, that we can see.

We'd rather hand out hot dogs in the name of Jesus to people who are homeless than address why they're homeless in the first place, because it's much less overwhelming. We'd rather provide housing to survivors of human trafficking, because building shelters is less complicated than building the economic resilience and social safety net of a community. We'd rather give a humanitarian a raise in salary than to address the cycle of burnout. Naturally, people need food, housing, and a fair income—but they need more than that too, something that may not come quite as easily as popping a coin into a vending machine.

But we still prefer the material. We give greater value to what we can see, to what is tangible—even when it comes to something as intangible as justice.

Much like the gross profit margin, sales growth, earnings per share, and other key performance indicators used by the corporate world, non-profits try to measure their impact in similar ways. This is no easy task—especially when it's monsoon season in Southeast Asia and flooding limits road access and slows down work productivity. Or when a disparity exists between what field workers consider to be long-lasting impact versus what the public values and is willing to read about on a website or in social media. Or when we don't know how to quantify things like raising self-esteem or building dignity or improving mental health or stabilizing emotional security.

We reduce our understanding of community transformation to digits and data. We view justice through infographics depicting the number of refugees receiving blankets or the percentage of villages that now have access to clean water or the decrease in reported cases of malaria. We don't care about the *how*—we just want to know *how many.*

Maybe the quantitative approach has a place in illustrating impact. But in my work, I've never felt that statistics alone can adequately convey how a life has changed.

This wasn't always the case for me. In my training as a student of human justice, social research methodology taught me that everything is measurable. And so when I spent my final semester of university as a practicum student in rural Mexico, I came with the expectation that the laws of cause and effect would apply. Insert efforts here; achieve powerful results here. But instead of gathering enough data for a momentous academic enterprise, my own definition of impact changed forever.

Initially, I was skeptical and disappointed when my supervisor in Mexico assigned me to work in a learning centre for children with special needs. Given that I had no training in teaching, the Spanish language, or special-needs education, I was bound to be challenged—except that it wasn't the sort of challenge I'd come to Mexico to pursue. Hard-wired for seeking scholastic success, I wanted to make calculable contributions that my academic community back in Canada would respect and value. Where was the merit in wiping runny noses and teaching the alphabet? How was I going to show my fellow practicum students and faculty members back home that I had made any sort of credible impact here?

I can't pinpoint the exact moment that everything changed, but I do know the exact cause. Her name was Julia, a beautiful six-year-old girl with Down's syndrome. She had a heart that was in no way proportionate to her physical size. And right from the beginning—with her contagious smile, her spirited personality, her silly sense of humour—she captured my heart.

While the rest of my peers back in Canada were writing policy in business suits, gaining hands-on experience with child and family services, or being trained to become professionals in the criminal justice system, I was wearing ripped jeans and an old T-shirt while teaching Julia how to ride a bicycle through the heat and grime of the Mexican desert. Every afternoon, the two of us would venture out into the macadamia nut orchard to practice pedaling—a formidable task for any beginner bicyclist learning to conquer the sandy resistance of Baja Californian roads, especially for someone who struggled with barriers to their motor skills.

All her life, people had underestimated Julia. Especially in the strong spiritual context in Mexico, having Down's syndrome not only meant she was "disabled" but also meant to many people that she was cursed. On one of my last afternoons in Mexico, however, Julia defied everybody's expectations of her physical capacity when she began cycling through dirt and sand all by herself, leaving me and the rest of her peers cheering behind her in a cloud of dust.

The joy and pride radiating on her face as she biked back toward me convinced me that some things in life can never be measured. Numbers are too flimsy. Even words can't fully describe the change that happened that day. Although it didn't translate to a gleaming bullet point on my resumé or a statistic I could impress my academic community with, I knew that moment was worth more than any kind of traditional achievement.

Giving It Time

Someone was murmuring a prayer in Greek as I held the hand of a young woman with a brown pixie haircut and a vacant expression. Down her arms and legs, she was covered in unsightly bruises from syringes that gave her access to the only coping mechanism she had left. She wavered now and then in her chair, still visibly high on the drugs she'd been able to purchase after servicing a client an hour or so before she'd come to see us at our drop-in centre. It wasn't because she was paid well that she could feed her addiction. It was more because buying drugs from the streets in this part of town was cheap, only about five euros—cheaper than a couple of orders of souvlaki.

In defiance of the jet leg and the heat, I forced myself to stay as present as possible while one of my fellow staff members prayed for the four women who came to attend our drop-in program that afternoon. As street workers in the red-light district of Athens, these women fell to the bottom of the prostitution hierarchy, earning the least money and experiencing the greatest degree of danger, violence, and abuse.

In this particular neighbourhood, trafficking was more easily observable than in any other red-light district I'd ever seen. Here, a wave of Bangladeshi women would arrive to these streets one month, wearing brightly coloured sarongs and smiles that weren't quite believable. The next month, it would be mostly Nigerian women robotically walking the trash-lined streets and working from sleazy rent-by-the-hour motels. Then the Bulgarians would come the month after that, and the Filipinos after that. The pattern of organized crime was never predictable here, but a pattern indeed existed.

The woman whose hand I was holding was from Romania, but she was hesitant to disclose to us how she'd come to Athens. She herself seemed confused and unclear on the details. The little I knew about her was that she was my age, although she had seen far more than I ever would in my lifetime. At only twenty-five, she had been working these streets for years, had grown addicted to drugs, and was HIV positive. And just the day before, she had discovered she was pregnant.

Yet again, I found myself in another one of those situations that felt hopeless. There I was, holding the hand of a woman who seemed too far beyond our reach—beyond anyone's reach.

"Pray for my baby," she told us upon announcing her pregnancy when she first walked into our drop-in centre, "and for me too."

I had no idea how to even start praying for this woman. It seemed too small a thing to do when her problems were so huge. Where did any of us begin with praying for her, let alone trying to help her?

When it comes to something as jarring as the trafficking and exploitation of human beings, we want to do something that will immediately solve the problem. We want to save; we want to fix; we want to abolish. And it's okay to want that, but the question is, *can we?* Can we really do all that by the press of a button—or by a one-time donation or a short-term mission trip? Surely we need those things too, but what we need even more than that is to stay committed for the long haul.

I suppose the frustrating but unchangeable thing about seeking justice—whether it's dealing with homelessness in our hometown, children with special needs in Mexico, or women coerced into prostitutions in Athens—is that it takes time.

Julia didn't start riding her bike the first day I met her. It took many months of building a relationship with her before she could trust me enough to let go and pedal on her own.

The journey from victim to survivor of human trafficking doesn't happen overnight. It comes through the cultivation of relationships built on trust, respect, and love; through rekindling self-worth and identity; through allowing the broken parts enough time and tenderness to heal.

As helpers, we've got to see ourselves less as saviours and more as cultivators, as if we were farmers. Before we reap a harvest, we need to plant and water and let things grow in a healthy environment. We prepare the land. We prune the plant. We get our hands dirty. We make ourselves vitally aware of the threat of natural disasters, but we are not deterred by them. And most of all, we patiently wait.

One of the more difficult parts about farming is that not all our crops will survive. Sometimes the plants we try to help grow are too much in the shade and lag behind the growth of other plants. Sometimes there are factors beyond our control—like storms or droughts that prevent our crops from growing at all.

That doesn't make our efforts wasted. That doesn't mean we've failed or that we're not cut out for farming. Most of all, that doesn't mean we should never try farming again, because nobody can do it perfectly.

There will always be obstacles in the way. We just need to give it time.

Greater Than the Tangible

Human nature desires to assign value to everything. The problem is that we don't always give value to things in the best way. We pay higher salaries to plastic surgeons, professional athletes, and sales managers than we do to teachers, pastors, farmers, and non-profit workers. We giver greater credence to an Ivy League alumni than to someone who has worked in the trenches for little or no pay. We think a country with a higher GDP must be better off than a country that treats its citizens with respect and dignity.

Metrics may play an important role, but they don't tell the whole story.

After spending a few months of teaching in Mexico, I returned to Canada with a recalibrated perspective of social impact. I discovered that sometimes justice is more than what is tangible, than what creates immediate results. It may not even come with words, not to mention a percentage or ratio or statistic. How do I describe what inspiring hope in a marginalized child in Mexico looks like? How can I convey the ground-breaking significance of showing love to someone who has only ever known abuse?

Some of the greatest things in the world cannot be given. You can give time, energy, donations, resources, and expertise, but you can't give justice—you seek it. You don't give freedom or happiness or self-esteem—you cultivate it. You inspire and mobilize it.

Justice is not quantifiable. It cannot be assessed by volume or mass or frequency or duration. It supersedes the confines of time and measurement, bearing far greater power and magnitude than its rival. Because justice takes time. Justice just is.

CHAPTER 4

We're Not Here to Judge:
Beyond Good Intentions

Teach me to hear that story through each person,
To cradle a sense of wonder in their life, to honour
the hard-earned wisdom of their sufferings,
To waken their joy that the King of all
kings stoops down to wash their feet,
And looking up into their face says, "I know - I understand."
—Caedmon

Light rain began falling from a darkened sky, so my friend Lauren˙ and I huddled under our hoods and protected the brown paper packages each of us carried. The biting winds of late November chilled us to the bone as we knocked hurriedly on the foggy glass door. People—men, mostly—shoved past us in the narrow cobblestone street, yet nobody seemed to be in as much of a rush as we were.

A gorgeous, dark-eyed woman quickly appeared at the door and ushered us inside. "Quick, come in," she urged us in a thick Eastern European accent. "You must be freezing!"

˙   Note: Name has been changed.

Lauren and I accepted the invitation gratefully, shutting the glass door behind us to keep out the cold air and the gawking men pointing suggestively and giving loud commentary. It was quieter inside, except for the predictable beats of nightclub music playing faintly from down the street. And it was much warmer too. A space heater aiming at the glass door blasted waves of artificial heat on its highest setting, giving us the momentary illusion of warmth.

"Elena*, your hair! It looks great. Did you dye it?" gushed Lauren, seeming unaffected by any level of discomfort from the situation.

Beaming from the compliment, Elena nodded and said in broken English, "Yes, yes, they let me go last week for haircut."

I silently noted the overtones of an external source of control in Elena's life. Although prostitution is legalized in Amsterdam, her obvious lack of freedom in her work was disconcerting to me. She spoke as if her every move was monitored and approved by someone else.

She also seemed so desperate for a regular social interaction with two other women who looked her in the eye and made small talk about hair salons and the changing weather. Never would she have such a "normal" conversation as this with a client. To them, she was little more than another dish at a buffet to be enjoyed and consumed.

It was my first red light district outreach, so I was almost too overcome by how bizarre and uncomfortable this new kind of situation was to be able to contribute much value to it. Yet Lauren and Elena chatted back and forth gregariously over the background noise while rowdy men made boisterous hoots and catcalls from the other side of the window. The two of them were either immune to this kind of behaviour, or they didn't bother to dignify the men with a reaction.

"What kind of soup did you bring tonight?" asked Elena with a hint of mixed excitement and impatience in her trembling voice. "I haven't eaten all day."

Lauren gave her the three options, and Elena pondered over them painstakingly, as if she were about to purchase a wedding dress or a new car. She seemed elated to have such a simple choice offered to her and finally decided on the meatball soup.

"It smells just like *ciorbă de perişoare*, the meatball soup my mother used to make in our family's restaurant in Bucharest," Elena said softly with a distant gaze that told me she was no longer speaking for our benefit. "I always imagined myself cooking there someday too. Maybe even owning that restaurant one day."

In a daze, she handed Lauren a few euros and thanked us profusely as we waved our goodbyes and got swallowed up by the crowd gathering outside her door. Without meeting the eyes of the noisy onlookers, she drew a red curtain across the interior of her glass parlour, momentarily separating herself from the reality she would be reacquainted with after her midnight dinner.

Stumbling over the uneven cobblestone streets in the dark, I accidentally bumped into a man with a black peacoat and a plaid scarf. With greying hair, distinguished glasses, and articulate speech, he could've been my history professor from university. He apologized, although his polite manners couldn't redeem the fact that he was lustfully gawking at the women in the windows as if they were consumable goods.

"Too bad she's off work now," he lamented, gesturing toward Elena's window. "I would've given her some business."

I couldn't hide the disgust on my face. Pushing past him wordlessly, Lauren and I hurried in the opposite flow of traffic to deliver our next soup orders.

No amount of academic research or behind-the-scenes office work for trafficking prevention agencies could've prepared me for that first night I met some of the women behind the windows of the infamous red light district in Amsterdam. Even with heavy layers of makeup, many of them looked more like girls than women to me. Behind a veil of glass, they stood on display as if they were mannequins placed strategically to usher in customers at a retail store. Wearing just enough fabric to cover some of their essentials while still advertising their wares, they posed their bodies with blank stares on cloudy faces, as if there was some detachment between mind and body.

And they wait.

The Backstory

On a crisp autumn day in Winnipeg, I was walking home from a coffee shop in a gritty neighbourhood when a man stopped me and asked if I had any spare change he could use for the laundromat. Given that the only change I had in my wallet were a few Thai baht coins after flying in from Southeast Asia a couple of days earlier, I had no spare change to give him. All I could offer him was using my credit card to buy him a sandwich from the Subway restaurant across the street.

"No, thank you, I ate some rice and beans already," he said politely after I made my offer. Then—without missing a beat—he asked, "Could you buy me a Coke instead?"

Nodding hesitantly, I felt pangs of guilt as we walked into Subway together to buy him something without a trace of omega-3s or antioxidants. *How far I've fallen as a humanitarian,* I thought begrudgingly, punishing myself for my decrescendo from working to improve the health of remote Cambodian villages a few days earlier to buying a homeless man a beverage with enough high fructose corn syrup to rot out all his teeth.

Handing him a bottle of Coke with a sheepish smile, I had to wonder if it was up to me to decide what this man actually needed. It was easy for me to assume he probably needed a healthy meal or a new jacket or anything else before he needed fifteen teaspoons of sugar in liquid form. But who was I to judge if this man had an occasional desire for a refreshing, non-alcoholic beverage, just as I crave a latté every now and then? Are only the middle and upper classes entitled to occasional indulgences, barring anyone else from enjoying the simple pleasures in life?

It's a common habit to judge someone begging on the streets, to presume that person is suffering from hunger or homelessness because of his or her own poor lifestyle choices. It's easy to walk past the windows displaying the women of the red light district in Amsterdam with the assumption that each one has willingly chosen to sell her body to strangers. But maybe it's not anyone's place to make brash inferences without knowing the story behind the story.

Many of the eleven million tourists that flock to Amsterdam each year[1] visit the infamous red light district to freely gape their way through streets that are the outcome of legalized prostitution. But while prostitution may be a legitimate source of income here, not everyone has entered this profession willingly. About 70 percent of these women are not from Amsterdam or even Holland.[2] Some of these women have been sold into slavery from Romania, Bulgaria, Hungary, North Africa, and South America. Many were economically devastated and were lured by a promise of employment that turned out to be a trap. Others were sold by their families in hopes of a better life elsewhere and a guaranteed source of income.

In blissful ignorance, hundreds of men pass by these women's glass cages every day, from as early as ten or eleven in the morning until well past midnight. They gawk, point, and catcall without reprisal, offering objectifying commentary among themselves: "Hey, look at *that* one! Do you see *those?* Check out *that.*" Men who otherwise hold respectable offices in society—counsellors, teachers, academics, business owners—come in throngs to Amsterdam and purchase a woman like a package of gum from the corner store.

Some women stand boldly, calling out to men on the streets to negotiate a fair price. Some shift uncomfortably beneath the glow of pink lighting, avoiding eye contact until a customer taps on the window with a fistful of euro banknotes and a lewd expression. Without showing signs of being under duress, she lets him in through the glass door. The red curtain is drawn. It's business as usual.

Behind every window is a woman with her own story. Maybe her reason for standing still and compliantly is because her pimp keeps such a watchful eye on her that her every move is monitored and controlled. Maybe she was trafficked from another country, and without legal documents or an understanding of the local language and culture, this seems to be her only option. Maybe she wasn't trafficked at all, but even though it was never her dream to become a sexual commodity in the marketplace, she had to make a choice of survival—which doesn't seem like much of a choice at all.

On that autumn day in Winnipeg, I didn't know how one man's life brought him to a place of asking for spare coins outside a Subway restaurant in the inner city. I don't know with certainty how Elena's dream of becoming a cook in Romania pivoted into renting a window in the red light district in Amsterdam, far away from her family in Bucharest. But in either case, it's not up to me to judge. All that's up to me is deciding how I'm going to help—and just as importantly, *why* I've chosen to help in the first place.

Hollow Humanitarianism

"Why are you here?"

Contemplative silence met the simple yet befuddling question. Thirty social justice professionals awkwardly shifted in their chairs, too nervous to answer incorrectly in case it was a trick question. Some of our group had flown all the way from

Virginia and Georgia into San Francisco for this two-week training session on aftercare services for survivors of human trafficking. Wasn't it obvious we were all here for the same reason?

"All right, I'll start," our trainer said after noting the unanimous sense of confusion in the room. "I'm here for this training because I love to teach." With some level of detachment, each person proceeded to share the same sort of predictable answer: *I'm here to learn. I'm here because I want to help. I'm here because I'm passionate about ending modern-day slavery.*

Nodding after the last person shared a one-line answer, our trainer thanked us and then bluntly said, "And now I want to hear why each of you are *really* here."

At the time, I was mildly offended by her insinuation that we could have ulterior motives for wanting to help trafficking survivors with their path to restoration. Fast-forwarding a few years later, however, when I was living among fellow expatriates in Cambodia, her question made more sense to me. Many of us share humanitarian aspirations. A lot of us come to countries like Cambodia because we want to learn and grow from exposure to a different culture. And those are the kinds of stories we love to share on Skype with our families or write about in the newsletters for our social circle back home.

But there is more to it than altruistic motives—there's a question of why we are *really* here. Sometimes, underneath that visible layer of wanting to "do good" as an ESL teacher, as an aid worker, as a missionary in Southeast Asia is the hidden thrill of being able to access an adventurous and reasonably comfortable lifestyle for dirt cheap—nice hotels for ten US dollars per night, elaborate meals for under four dollars, inexpensive flights to vacation in Indonesia and Thailand. There's the affirmation from our Facebook friends who ooh and aah over the pictures we post of us with a gaggle of adorable barefoot Cambodian children clinging on to us affectionately.

To our friends and family back home, doing aid work in Cambodia elevates us to a level of moral supremacy and virtuoso. And that's problematic for a few reasons—not only because it creates an unrealistic standard for us to attain but also because there's always a backstory for why we've chosen to be in the place we're at.

The upsetting truth is that there are always people who end up doing aid work in Cambodia for terrible reasons. Some end up there because of all the things they can get away with in a virtually lawless society with a dysfunctional government. Twentysomething expatriate males called "sexpats" sleaze their way through the city streets of Siem Reap and Phnom Penh, trawling bars and massage parlours where they can purchase sex with young women—and sometimes even boys—for disturbingly cheap and with impunity. Of course, not every expat I've met chose to move to Cambodia with malicious intent. Not every humanitarian I met came with some neo-colonial agenda. But all of us had our own story, and few had the courage to share the entirety of it.

Within a world where you'd expect to find only selflessness, there is ego. There is self-gratification. I've worked for non-profit agencies that turned out to value their image more than anything else. They spent more time hosting black-tie galas for elite donors and more money on filming flashy promotional videos than they ever did on rebuilding the communities they claimed to be helping.

Let's be honest: even humanitarians care about status. It's just a different kind of status. When our identity as humanitarians is adjudicated on the grounds of morality and nobility, it's inevitable that we're going to strive for perfection—and to be acknowledged for it too. Not only do we want to represent justice well, but we also want to represent ourselves well. We want to be the holiest missionary, the most risk-taking relief worker, the most zealous humanitarian. Ironically enough, sometimes we even take pride in how humble we try to be.

Seeking status over seeking justice is hollow. It's hollow because status changes, image fades, and self-gratification is fleeting. Being present only to receive the rewards is a dangerous reason to be part of the justice movement—because what happens when there are more struggles than achievements?

Here's the hard truth: it doesn't always feel good to do the just thing. It can seem like thankless, even pointless work. Sometimes we invest so much and reap so little.

I know that feeling well. While working at an inner city youth drop-in centre, I had my wallet stolen by the same people I was trying to help. A few weeks later, somebody torched the playground of that same drop-in centre to ashes—and people wondered why we bothered to work in a neighbourhood that was so far gone, so ungrateful, so prone to rejecting our help. Never did I hear my boss congratulate me on work well done at that job. Rarely did I hear a word of appreciation from the people I served. And on my way to and from work every day for months, I would give a granola bar to Ernie, a homeless man who sat on the same patch of sidewalk along my route, who never once grunted a word of thanks to me.

I've had to learn quickly that the humanitarian sphere is not the place to be if my expectation is to feel appreciated and celebrated. If I've committed to seeking justice, I've got to be okay with making sacrifices without ever receiving a pat on the back.

The truth is, the rewards don't always come after a week or two months or even a year of service. If they do come after the long haul, seeking justice doesn't necessarily yield the personal return on investment we want. It doesn't always culminate in profound success stories or endless feel-good moments of satisfaction from a job well done. Sometimes the success story is as simple and mundane as going through a whole day without a major crisis. Sometimes, instead of accolades and recognition, we're given deep scars and disillusioned discoveries. We endure fragmented suffering that may only ever make sense in retrospect—if ever at all.

Gratification can't be the ultimate goal of seeking justice. So does that make it wrong to pursue justice with some level of self-interest? And if we do act justly with hopes for fulfilling, feel-good moments, does our self-interest invalidate our work? I don't think so. We may love somebody for millions of reasons about them, but is that love nullified if part of us loves out of a desire to receive love back? Maybe not. I think the love still counts. And I think every effort in the direction of freedom and justice counts too. After all, as humans, do we *ever* act out of pure selflessness?

We just need to be careful. We need to be responsible for how we choose to live out our convictions.

Just as it isn't my place to judge how a woman ended up working in the red light district in Amsterdam, it also isn't up to me to determine whether or not the person wanting to help her has valid intentions. My own reasons for choosing a vocation in social justice aren't anybody's business but my own, either. However, that doesn't minimize the relevance of my intentions.

My intentions don't need to be as noble as trying to save the melting Arctic or as grandiose as wanting to rescue every last slave forced to work against his or her will. My intentions don't have to be based on what's expected of me, given my role as a pastor's daughter or the fact I was born into a family of professional caregivers. If I look beyond the surface level, beyond the finite; if my efforts see the soul of humans instead of judging them as victims; if I intend to do good instead of harm—then that's the kind of help that can make a meaningful difference.

Helping the Helper

As of 2009, there were over 1.4 million registered charities and foundations in the United States alone.[3] Based only on quantity, it seems there is no shortage of movement done in the name of justice. What a number like this doesn't tell us, however, is how much of it accounts for good work and how much of it is purely good intentions that failed to follow through.

Good intentions and good work may be drawn from the same source, but they're two different things. Good intentions are often based on emotional impulses and result in action with minimal effort. Good intentions look like the kind but not-so-well-planned gestures of churches and charities shipping off crates of used clothing to people in Uganda or Malawi. Good work, on the other hand, is willing to hear the whole story of that community in Uganda or Malawi first. It recognizes that Western groups sending cast-off clothing overseas has been undercutting the African textile and garment industry at the local level for years and that maybe the solutions lie within the people who are most affected to begin with.

The white-saviour complex driving these well-intentioned efforts is often what causes the harm. It's trying to give a voice to someone who already has one and speaking on their behalf. It's believing dignity is something we can transfer to a survivor of human trafficking in Atlanta or a subsistence farmer in Tajikistan, as if it were as easy as slipping them some cash. Good work, on the other hand, understands that survivors of trafficking or farmers in developing countries have the agency to speak for themselves and that the world needs to hear the whole story from her or from him, not from you or me. Most of all, good work accepts that no human was meant to carry the burden of trying to be a saviour—that's God's job.

Usually we create unintended harm when we make assumptions about people's needs without consulting them directly or without working collaboratively. We illustrate a limited portrayal of the kind of person who qualifies for help. We categorize people as either heroes or victims. We assign terms like *needy* and *vulnerable* to a certain demographic, suggesting that we don't *all* experience seasons of neediness and vulnerability, regardless of income. We love to pray over the "poor," as if the rest of us have it all together.

We even divide people into levels of neediness. Ever since the Victorian era, we've developed a sense of the "deserving" and "undeserving" poor. The "deserving" are the orphans and widows, the single moms working four jobs to feed their kids, the bloated African children we see in World Vision commercials with protruding rib cages and flies crawling over their faces. Meanwhile, the "undeserving" are the hoodlums and teenage gang members, the drug-addicted criminals, the sex-trade workers, the ones who drink away their days instead of finding a job. All of these are people who are in need of some form of help, but we're quick to judge the latter group as too lazy or ignorant to be worthy of a loving intervention.

By dichotomizing those who need or deserve help and those who don't, we set up humanitarian work to be paternalistic. It becomes a one-sided relationship, creating a power imbalance where the humanitarian gets to judge *who* needs help and *how* to help them.

Who, then, helps the helper? Does this mean that the hopeless cycle of addictions, the devastating breakdown of family, or the experience of abuse in a middle-class, university-educated family in a developed country doesn't count as a trial or hardship? Maybe we're all struggling with different things in the same world, all of us in need of love and grace, all of us wanting forgiveness and redemption.

The truth is, we're all broken. All of us. People who have experienced human trafficking may be broken by trauma, not only from their exploitation but also often from trauma originating early in their childhoods. The pimps and companies that exploit people's labour, the johns and pornography addicts that fuel human trafficking—they're broken too, from something that is leading them to cope or survive in empty ways. The helpers, missionaries, and humanitarians are also broken. They're broken by past victimization, desires to be more lovable and worthy, beliefs of needing to carry the heaviest cross to be "holy enough," or efforts to redeem themselves from the wrongs they've committed in the past.

Whether we identify as a victim or survivor of abuse, a law-abiding citizen or a gang member, we're broken in some way. Broken by addictions and bad choices. Broken by hurtful and abusive relationships. Broken by loss and unresolved issues from the past. Broken by our mistakes and haunting regrets and painful failures. Broken by trials we didn't ask for and sometimes by thrusting ourselves into challenging situations to prove our worth. Broken because of healing we've desperately prayed for that has never come.

Everyone is broken. And maybe all of us—including those who are resource-poor or suffering—have something to offer too.

For myself as a teacher for kids with special needs, I came with a tenacious desire to serve my students with all my heart, without expecting my students to reciprocate. On my last day of teaching, however, I boarded the school bus with a heavy heart to take my students home one final time. Under the cover of darkness, I let down my guard as my body silently shook from half-suppressed sobs. I was a puddle of tears. Suddenly, the frail, bony arms of a twelve-year-old girl with cerebral palsy encircled my waist in a comforting embrace. She gave me exactly what I needed—something I couldn't do for myself. She who had little material wealth to give ended up giving me the most invaluable gift: the gift of human connection, the kind that let me know I'm heard and loved and not alone.

In the end, our work comes down not to being humanitarian heroes but to being wholly human. It's about relationships. It's about community. It's the mutual desire to help and to respect, the shared learning, the common humanity that is the core of justice.

Common Humanity

Back in that lecture hall in San Francisco, it was when everyone spoke their story and the truth of their intentions that the distinction between "us" as humanitarians and "them" as victims of human trafficking was blurred. No longer was the room populated with superhuman world-changers. By admitting there was more to our stories, we could find the humility to accept that perhaps all of us were in need of help— just different kinds of help. A desire for helping to heal the brokenness in the life of a survivor dwelled within the same person who also craved to find healing, worthiness, and love.

Instead of our social justice hierarchy, there was raw humanity. There were feelings of guilt. Beliefs of undeserved privilege and senses of obligation. Feelings of pride and perfectionism. Repression. Desires for personal redemption. Inadequacy and worries of being unlovable. Over-identification with survivors and unnecessary feelings of responsibility for their strife. Assumptions that a humanitarian identity was what validated self-worth and gained the respect of others.

That's when we need to figure our what our deepest intentions are. Because acting out of guilt leaves us unfulfilled. Acting out of obligation leaves us resentful. Acting out of pride leaves us empty.

We're not here to judge—we're here to help. Our first task is not to fix—it's to listen. Our job is not to determine whether someone is or isn't worthy of helping—it's to see we're all in need of grace and unconditional love. Our purpose is not to evaluate if someone else has good-enough intentions for wanting to help—it's to accept that we're all imperfect. The only judgment left up to us is to judge ourselves and our own intentions.

Yes, it may be less painful to try fixing the brokenness in other people rather than addressing the brokenness we conceal in ourselves. It may be easier to try solving the problems in other countries than to confront the injustices permeating our own borders. But it's time to shift the conversation. It's time to start identifying our need to be rescued and redeemed from our own pain and dysfunctions before trying to rescue and redeem others.

As we talk about wanting to change the world, we need to talk about how we can change ourselves.

---

[1] "Record Number of Tourists in Netherlands in 2011," Amsterdam Herald, February 2, 2012, http://amsterdamherald.com/index.php/allnews-list/124-20120202-tourism.

[2] Licia Brussa, ed., Sex Work in Europe (Amsterdam: TAMPEP International Foundation, 2009), 20.

3   Katie L. Roeger, Amy Blackwood, and Sarah L. Pettijohn, "The Nonprofit Sector in Brief: Public Charities, Giving, and Volunteering," Urban Institute, November 1, 2011, http://www.urban.org/uploadedpdf/412434-nonprofitalmanacbrief2011.pdf.

CHAPTER 5

Half-Hearted Justice:
When Compassion Isn't Enough

The whole history of the progress of human liberty shows
that all concessions yet made to her august claims have
been born of earnest struggle … Those who profess to
favour freedom and yet depreciate agitation are [people]
who want crops without plowing up the ground; they
want rain without thunder and lightning. They want the
ocean without the awful roar of its many waters.
—Frederick Douglass

A red sun spread its hazy reflection across the secluded bay
of the South China Sea, its rays reaching toward me in a warm
embrace while driving away a cast of crabs into the shadows
of palm trees. Steady saltwater waves rolled melodically into
the bay, pushing fields of foam that quenched the shores of
the white-sand beach. And I was the sole proprietor of this
abandoned beach—the only one awake early enough to be
spellbound by nature's morning majesty.

It was a time for replenishing. After several months of managing
human trafficking prevention programs in rural Cambodia, I
could no longer evade how the grim realities of my work were
gnawing away at my soul. I opted for a reclusive, one-week

vacation on an island off the coast of Malaysia, aching for restoration with the most desperate sort of hope.

I needed respite as much as I needed oxygen. Every night on that island, I would lie in the humid heat while staring at the rotating ceiling fan in my one-room thatch hut, listening to the waves gently lapping, wondering how long the healing was going to take. In mid-prayer, I'd fall asleep while begging God for this island to be the elixir I needed to return to my work with renewed strength.

And so, after several turbulent months in the squalid border town I lived in back in Cambodia, I spent my waking hours sitting on the beach in quiet gratitude for this temporary piece of peace. I savoured the soul-soothing moments of silent solitude just as much as I enjoyed marvelling at the rugged island's jungle-covered granite peaks fringed by white beaches and azure waters.

On that particular morning, as the sun ascended further above the sea's technicolour coral reefs and the island's emerald clusters of palm trees, I started realizing how lonely I was. It wasn't because I was a travelling nomad with a wayfaring soul, sitting alone on an island in Malaysia. It was a lonesomeness that came from feeling as if I lived in a world that seemed content with turning on axes of evil, greed, and apathy. And in a few moments, that feeling was about to multiply and leave me lonelier than I'd ever been before.

Sandals dangling in hand, a middle-aged American woman came strolling toward me in the middle of my musing and greeted me congenially in a thick New York accent. Without my soliciting for it, she delved into her story of leaving NYC on a quest to "find herself," which she seemed to think would happen somewhere in Southeast Asia's humid tropics. After explaining that even the Buddhist monks in Thailand couldn't help her locate her identity and sent her to consult with the imams in Malaysia, she turned the conversation to me and asked, "So, what kind of work do you do?"

I was torn between telling the truth and giving a fabrication of it. The moment I'd boarded my plane from Siem Reap to Kuala Lumpur for this vacation, I'd vowed to myself that I would give my tired mind a temporary reprieve from pondering over safe-migration campaigns and sustainable-livelihood strategies to mitigate human trafficking. Vaguely, I mentioned my work in human trafficking prevention with hope that she wouldn't demand a longer commentary.

Her face became immediately crestfallen. Gathering herself together, she told me in a hushed, wavering voice, "That's why I had to get out of Thailand as fast as I could and come here. I was so heartbroken and tired of watching children being abused over there."

When It's Easier to Feel Than to Do

Nothing inhibits justice more than ignorance and silence.

When my fellow traveller told me she had run away from the same problem I was fighting against, I was disappointed—yet not surprised. It was that classic case of being convicted by a justice issue enough to feel sorrowful but not quite enough to do anything about it.

I've been there. Sometimes I'm still there.

Less than half a decade earlier, I'd perceived human trafficking much like the New Yorker I met in Malaysia. I'd felt all the right feelings a person should feel about it: sadness and sorrow, guilt and grief, indignation and infuriation … I'd believed that, like any other breach of human rights, modern slavery was wrong, although it had been little more than a distressing abstraction to me.

I could've watched every documentary on the growing epidemic of modern slavery and have the same dewy-eyed laments about human trafficking with my equally impassioned friends. I could've abided by the clichéd pattern of attending every social justice conference, carrying placards at every rally, shedding tears at every candlelit vigil. Aside from a little bit of time, it would've cost me next to nothing—but it would've produced next to nothing too.

Believing is one thing. Spurring beliefs into motion is something completely different. Beliefs are safe, harmless. They aren't risky or dangerous. They don't inconvenience anyone or require sacrifices. But beliefs alone also don't solve problems or counter evil.

Compassion is important, but on its own, it's limited. Watching BBC news with a box of tissues is not going to end child labour, pull twelve-year-old girls out of the brothels they were sold into, or feed the homeless person who hangs out by the Dumpster in the back alley. All the feelings of empathy and all the passionate convictions and strong-willed beliefs of right and wrong in the world may make me feel good about myself, but they're not setting anyone free.

Compassion is comfortable—activism hurts. Compassion gives off an illusion of altruism without having to do any of the work—activism means labouring tirelessly, anonymously, and thanklessly. Compassion demands for so little—activism asks for so much.

From migrant workers in the deserts of Mexico, to Romany families forced to live in ghettos because of racism in Hungary and Bulgaria, to subsistence farmers in rural Cambodia, most of the people I've met in vulnerable situations would much prefer for me to act than to be filled with sympathy and good intentions. They don't want pity. If anything, they want help—the kind of help that makes sense in their context.

Choosing to do more than feel badly about human trafficking has instigated radical changes in my life. Instead of hearing stories of survivors of human trafficking from a safe distance, I transitioned to working so deep in the trenches that I could identify with their pain. It became so real and so relevant that the divide between "me" and "them" was blurred, and heroism became inconsequential.

And so, on that island in Malaysia, when I encountered somebody who chose to turn away from the glaring reality of human trafficking, I was both understanding and indignant. Just like her, I've never had an affinity for watching people at the margins of society suffer from the inescapable cycle of exploitation. At the same time, choosing to battle against forced labour, sexual slavery, and child labour wasn't because I found it particularly enjoyable but rather because there is a tremendous need. Feeling overwhelmed with pity after stumbling upon child exploitation in Southeast Asia shouldn't be a reason to withdraw but an invitation to help, a reason to stay, a chance to learn and give and grow.

In the fight against human trafficking—or any other injustice, for that matter—we need all the help we can get, not for people to shield their eyes and run away. When people plead ignorance in order to be excused from any moral obligations to act justly, the problem doesn't go away; it gets worse.

As soon as we disconnect compassion from action, it's too easy to relegate compassion to a purely emotional sphere, pat ourselves on the back for feeling sorrow for somebody in pain, and then move on—which is pity, not mercy. Or we intellectualize it: we try to understand it, reason with it, explain it, evaluate it, plan it—and eventually, talk ourselves out of it.

On its own, compassion isn't enough. It isn't the final destination. Compassion is a starting point—a catalyst for good work to be done.

When It's Easier to Not Feel at All

When an illegally built garment factory crumbled to the ground in the spring of 2013 near Dhaka, Bangladesh, causing over one thousand fatalities, the world stood still in shock.

Bangladeshi garment factories are notorious hotspots for exploitation. With a $20 billion garment industry, the country is saturated by the factories of popular American retailers that eagerly flock here for cheap business in a virtually unregulated industry. This too was the case in the Dhaka collapse, and subsequent investigations of the factory building exposed cases of slave labour.

When I read the news, I was devastated on multiple levels. Such a catastrophic event is one to be mourned in its own right. But the cynic in me felt just as devastated that it took a disaster of such cataclysmic proportions before our world flinched at the underlying issues of systemic exploitation. Once the impassioned rampage of the International Labour Organization and other major human rights advocates were given their airtime, I wondered how much of a mourning period our collective attention span would permit before reverting back to celebrity gossip and sports news, only to be jolted again by the next global catastrophe.

Sure enough, by the time Typhoon Haiyan hit the Philippines a few months later that year, the tragedy in Bangladesh seemed to be forgotten.

Disasters like the one in Dhaka are not new phenomena. This one horrifying incident in Bangladesh only helps to shed another inch of light on the age-old injustice that has proven to be virtually resilient to anti-slavery laws ever since the Age of Abolition in the 1700s. More and more, cases of forced labour are being revealed. Human trafficking is quickly becoming the justice issue of this generation, hitting the radar of non-profits, government agencies, social media, and the international community unlike never before. It's something we're starting to talk about, something we feel horribly about, but it's also something few of us are actively invested in.

And it's no wonder. It's too hard to spend much mental and emotional energy dwelling on the natural disasters and human-made evil of the world. My mind can't even grasp the thousand deaths and countless people exploited in Dhaka or the 35.8 million people in slavery throughout the world.[1] I hear about the legacy of conflict in Palestine and Israel, Syria and Egypt, but it seems too complicated for me to understand, too far away to compel my involvement, and too systemically entrenched for me to do anything about it anyhow.

When all I hear on the news is racial tensions and violence in the United States, malnutrition in Africa, tsunamis obliterating the coasts of Southeast Asia, and poverty on every inch of the globe, where do I start? I can care, I can pray, I can read about it and learn about it and talk about it, yet it's hard to feel I could possibly make any kind of impact.

Some days, I don't want to know more information about human trafficking. I don't want to hear the most recently updated estimation of slaves in the world—because whether it's twenty-seven million or thirty-six million, it's still going to be such a big, overwhelming, depressing number that I'll feel too small to do anything about it. There are days I wish I was less aware, that I could disappear back into the fantasy world I used to live in as a child, where social justice activism was as simple as raking yards for senior citizens. Days I'd rather burrow myself in shallow entertainment as respite and let apathy win than to give one more piece of my heart to grieving another epidemic. Another terrorist attack. Another miscarriage of justice.

Sometimes compassion is easier than activism. But there are plenty of times when even compassion is too hard to handle.

When the presence of injustice becomes overwhelming, our natural reaction is to avoid. When the six o' clock news features famine and poverty, we switch channels. When world affairs rise into conversation, we're tempted to give our minds a break by changing topics. We avoid visiting parts of town or travelling to other countries where human suffering is unconcealed in order to protect ourselves from guilt.

It gets even more difficult to face tragedies when we know we *could* be doing something about it. There's a little less responsibility in talking about how brutal human trafficking is in India and Nepal than to confront how much it happens in our own backyard in North America. It's a little less personal to talk about slavery when sex tourists are the culprits rather than to admit that we're fuelling labour trafficking by purchasing cheap goods made by slaves. It's inconvenient knowing we need to make changes in our daily lives by seeking out ethically made products in order to practice spending habits that support human freedom and dignity.

We may choose to turn either toward or away from human trafficking, poverty, abuse, and gender-based violence, but as William Wilberforce once remarked, "we can never again say that we did not know."

Awareness Is a Starting Point, Not an Ending Point

My fellow traveller from New York infuriated me for wanting to avoid the same problem I had devoted my life to mitigating. But she also helped raise a few questions. Her woefulness about the treatment of children in Thailand led me to ask myself, *Is it ever okay to feel helpless in a world that grieves?*

I'll never forget the first time I saw the frail frames and stunted bodies of children begging for spare coins and food along the Thai border. Or when I crossed the bloodstained floors of Tuol Sleng, a high school that Pol Pot had turned into a torture, interrogation, and execution centre during the Cambodian genocide. Or that sickening moment at Dachau concentration camp when I walked through the gas chambers, which once had been used to execute up to four hundred prisoners at one time. In those moments, I didn't feel inspired to fight against poverty or to prevent genocide—I felt completely disempowered.

Sometimes the helplessness sets in because some problems *are* too big for us to solve alone.

It certainly felt that way many times when I worked with underprivileged inner city who seemed as if they'd never turn away from belligerent and self-destructive behaviours. I had many hopeless days of working alongside children with special needs, knowing they may never learn to verbally communicate. I know the mournful frustration of dishing out meals at a soup kitchen, seeing the same faces every day and wondering if the cycle of hunger and poverty will ever be broken.

The problems of the world *should* leave us frightened and disheartened. We need to allow ourselves enough time to feel the feelings and to emotionally react and even retract in order to know what kind of an injustice we're up against. Time gives us the space we need to ensure we aren't responding out of guilt, which is never a good motivator. Problems need to be scary enough that we're concerned—but not too intimidated to evade action.

So maybe it's okay to watch the news and feel helpless about countries being ravaged by earthquakes and tsunamis. Maybe it's not such a bad thing to be overwhelmed by the numbers of people who are enslaved and exploited, malnourished and moneyless, diseased and dying—numbers that never go away, only seeming to get bigger. It's all part of the process that leads us to choose what we're going to do about it.

Awareness isn't final, but it's certainly foundational. Compassion on its own is only an emotion unless it becomes a catalyst for acting. And action isn't transformational unless it's attached to mercy, motivated by love, and propelled by community.

Practicing Compassion-Fuelled Action

From my own experience in the social justice field, compassion counts for something. But on its own, it's not enough. A twinge of sorrow on behalf of an exploited garment worker or a child forced into domestic servitude isn't going to advance anybody's freedom. But acting without compassion is dangerous too. It risks the giver working too hard and burning out, leaving the receiver with loveless handouts.

Mercy and justice were never meant to be mutually exclusive.

Some of the people in developing countries I've met want help to come from a wholehearted human, not an institution. They want help from someone who will try to understand their pain by taking the time to hear their stories, their struggles—not slap a Band-Aid on the problem. They want someone who is willing to support their ideas of how to heal brokenness in their communities, instead of unanimously implementing foreign ideas without consultation. Someone who doesn't see "me" or "them"—just "us." Someone whose actions aren't mechanical or governed by guilt but rooted in love and respect.

We need that feeling of compassion that precedes justice and stirs us to a tangible response. But the feeling is not separate from the act itself, nor can the response be devoid of the emotion. If we're purely guided by emotion, we can expect to be exhausted and burned out before long. And if we're only driven by a compulsion to work, then we may forget why we started working in the first place.

Mercy without movement is futile and feeble—it makes me one who pities. Action without empathy is heartless—it makes me one who indoctrinates. Seeking compassion-fuelled justice is what makes me one who helps.

---

1   Walk Free Foundation, "The Global Slavery Index 2014," Global Slavery Index, accessed November 15, 2014, http://www. globalslaveryindex.org/.

CHAPTER 6

The Sound of Silence:
Paralysis by Analysis

You may choose to look the other way,
But you can never again say you did not know.
—William Wilberforce

It was one of the hottest days of the summer in Cambodia and the most inauspicious time to bring a team of refined Western donors as far away from air conditioning as possible. Yet without complaint or hesitation, our conspicuous team of khaki-wearing Caucasians trekked by foot through the waves of heat and clouds of dust kicked up by motorbikes and tractors hauling oversized loads of rice. With zealous intent, our group waged forward to reach some of our most rural project sites.

With a mix of sorrow and intrigue, the team of donors asked us about the well-trodden, illegal border crossings to Thailand we walked past. They wanted to know the fate of undocumented migrant labourers who searched for work on the other side of the border, cringing when we said that many of them returned with brain injuries and physical disabilities from being beaten by unscrupulous employers. With disbelief, the donors shook their heads as our team informed them that sometimes these migrants never returned at all.

Like most first-time visitors to Cambodia, the donor group seemed too torn between helplessness and hopefulness to choose either reaction. Exposing them to the horrific realities of human trafficking in northwestern Cambodia was overwhelming for them—and that was precisely why we came to show them how our team was working to mitigate it.

My staff and I explained that a major cause of human trafficking in rural Cambodia was a lack of decent job opportunities. We pointed out the chicken coops our staff helped to construct alongside families who were desperately searching for an alternative income source to illegally migrating to Thailand for work. We introduced them to one of the village leaders we'd trained so that he could teach his community how to protect themselves against traffickers. We brought them to meet a group of twenty women we'd mentored to create a savings-and-loan group to provide an extra layer of economic security.

No matter how well we showcased the impact our staff had in these villages, though, none of it would matter to this donor group if they found even the slightest flaw in our work. Because for many people, when it comes to seeking justice, it doesn't seem worth the effort whenever there's a possibility for failure.

As we headed back to the bus, the visitors marvelled at the speed and dexterity of six-year-old boys scaling palm trees to tap for sugar, at the height of the loads that women in colourful sarongs carried on their heads as they strolled barefoot down the dirt street. They asked about the wooden houses built on stilts and how children managed to study inside their homes at night without electricity.

Then one of the donors pointed with curiosity and asked about a concrete silo with a blue spout, next to one of the huts. Motioning for the team to examine it from up close, I explained that the concrete silo was a water-filtration system called a bio-sand filter, which our organization had supplied for the family. As I peered inside the filter to demonstrate the filtration process, my heart skipped a beat. I was thrown off by the unsightly mound of crumpled plastic bags and discarded cans of Angkor beer that concealed the carefully designed system of layered rocks for filtration.

Blankly, I looked at my translator for answers. She turned to the owners of the filter, who were staring from nearby while swaying from netted hammocks hanging in the shade beneath their house on stilts. After a brief exchange of words in Khmer, my translator turned back to me, looking quite embarrassed.

"Well, uh," she explained hesitantly, "they say they're using it as a garbage can now."

Unintended Harm

Never have I been much of a physics buff. Yet after my years in the social justice arena, Newton's law of motion has become increasingly relevant to me. Suppose his theory about objects applies to me: that each of my actions as a humanitarian has an equal and opposite reaction. If that's the case, then that must mean there will always be the possibility for that reaction to have detrimental consequences.

Viewing ethical pursuits through the lens of this taunting theory by Newton, I sometimes feel more debilitated than empowered. There is always a fear that my efforts to do good will provoke something bad. And so, with every bake-sale fundraiser I attend where proceeds are donated to education projects in West Africa, I feel as though we're undoing our benevolence, knowing that most of the chocolaty ingredients in the baked goods were harvested by unpaid and exploited children in Ghana and the Ivory Coast. I quickly lose that sense of solidarity and purpose I used to feel at these kinds of events, because I feel as though we're doing more harm than good.

Every time I attend churches that send hand-me-down T-shirts and shoes to clothe children in Africa, my heart no longer swells from these acts of charity. Because as well intentioned these motives may be, the consequences are slowly devastating the local textile industry in countries like Kenya, Uganda, and Nigeria. While giving gifts of clothes may keep them warm or protect them from the scorching sun, we're undercutting their ability to build their own workforce, and we end up creating an economic dependency.

And like many Westerners, I've joined the ranks of people who believe food should be fair trade, organic, and healthy. But the decisions I make for my own health often come at the expense of somebody else. Participating in the organic health foods movement sometimes means purchasing imported foods, such as quinoa, from the Global South. Now countries like Bolivia and Honduras struggle to afford the skyrocketed price of their own locally grown staple foods while Western nations stock their shelves with it.[1] How do we balance this trade-off? How do we be healthy *and* responsible without compromising someone else's well-being?

Inquisitive minds that critique, analyze, and investigate and have just as much potential to be constructive as counterproductive. Somebody needs to have the acumen and audacity to ask the tough questions that challenge our purchasing behaviours, the ethics of charitable giving, and the integrity of non-profit organizations. Seldom do we benefit, however, when the questioning only produces an endless stream of questions, the analyzing becomes immobilizing, or the investigating leads to stone-cold bitterness and resentment.

In my case, my habit of criticism grew into a staunch state of mind. I grew skeptical of everything. I felt deeply discouraged by charitable fundraisers, like bikeathons and twenty-four-hour fasts and 10k team races, which seemed to be all it took to make a school or church feel fulfilled in changing the world. I cringed at child-sponsorship programs in developing countries, wondering if it was more about having a child's picture on the refrigerator to make us feel good and look good whenever we have company over. I was no longer convinced that fair trade was as much about justice as it was about amplifying the trendiness of consumerism by creating guilt-free purchases, as if it were a fashionable genre of humanitarianism. I dismissed the possibility that wearing a bracelet for a cause, hitting "like" on Facebook, or signing my name on a petition was the best way to work toward justice—or that it was even about justice at all.

Something's got to be wrong, I thought, *if all it takes is a two-hour shift at the soup kitchen once a year at Thanksgiving or a two-week mission trip to dig a well in Kenya to quench humanitarian desires.* To me, all this seemed more like a fun way to represent a cause rather than a committed way of *being* the cause.

Hypocrisy was everywhere, or so I thought. I grew angry with churches proclaiming to stand for human rights and freedom that then, after the service, served pots of coffee sourced by exploited labourers working in hazardous conditions in Guatemala. I shook my head at schools that posted the UN's declaration of child rights to education, leisure, and dignity on the walls and in the classrooms while dotting their hallways and cafeterias with vending machines dispensing chocolate bars made by child slaves.

Finding flaws in every route for social justice eventually led me to a place of believing no possibilities were worth pursuing. Either it was too simple or too convoluted; too prone to failure or not risky enough. Everything was defective. The only option remaining was bitterness, which wasn't much of an option at all.

Paralysis by Analysis

Navigating my way through disillusionment has brought me to two equally valid conclusions that need to be balanced: it's important to be conscientious and critically aware, but it's just as important to not overthink compassion either.

Regressing to the gloomy silence of cynicism is understandable after seeing an expensive water filter being used as a garbage can. Or after realizing we provided the wrong kind of physical therapy for a child in a wheelchair. Or after watching countless organizations teaching English to remote African tribes who never asked to learn a language so irrelevant to them in the first place.

It's easier to be cynical than to keep moving forward in spite of resistance, with criticisms in check. It's more comfortable to have an opinion than to act on it. It's less demanding to dismiss a possibility than try to improve it.

Critical thinking can develop into a sort of paranoia when prospective actions are divided into black-and-white outcomes of either good or bad. For myself as a perfectionist, if there's any chance my efforts might produce negative consequences, then I'd rather not make the effort at all. I criticize the social justice movement to the point of pushing myself into paralysis by analysis: I think my way out of reacting.

There are so many occasions I succumb to paralysis by analysis, but none more frequent than when I'm confronted with homelessness in my own neighbourhood. Shamefully, when I meet somebody begging for food or money on the street, my first instinct isn't always compassion. Sometimes I silently judge my way through the encounter instead: *If I give her food, will it encourage her to keep begging instead of seeking dignified employment? If I give him money, will he spend it on drugs or other addictive habits? Will I be paying a trafficker's wage if this is a situation of forced begging or slavery?*

This confusing cloud of questions continues to swirl in my head until I have already passed him or her by. I've made a decision by default and missed out on an opportunity to do good.

I'm learning to be critical—but I also need to be critical of being critical.

Conviction first came to me on a lonely evening in Cambodia. It was a routine night of cooking dinner beside a feebly rotating fan in the quiet, empty house I lived in by myself. My thoughts drifted from slicing eggplant to thinking about the guard who was stationed twenty-four hours a day at my housing complex. His job wasn't pleasant. During his two-week shifts, he monitored the safety of our complex without being permitted to leave. Knowing his salary was minimal and he only had a hot plate to cook his meals, I decided to make supper for two that night.

As I cooked, my mind drifted to the snags in my plan. It occurred to me that few Cambodians were vegetarians like me—would he even want to eat a meal without meat? Would he be repulsed by tofu or by my cooking? What if he had already eaten? What if he was taking a nap and I would be interrupting his sleep? What if I ended up doing him a disservice?

Slowly, without even consciously realizing it, I was talking myself out of kindness on the presumption that I wouldn't actually be helpful. I was letting my doubts decide for me.

But then I thought about all the moments I had secretly hoped a Good Samaritan would cross my path in my own times of need or uncertainty. I thought of all the occasions I'd experienced that sinking feeling of needing encouragement or comfort and receiving none. How lonely did it feel during my darkest seasons of silently crying out for somebody to rescue me but having nobody come to my aid?

I'd been on both sides. I have wanted to send an email to build up a friend but decided against it because I thought my words would be misconstrued or seem too preachy. I have considered gently approaching that person on the bus who seemed to be having a terrible day but decided it would be too invasive to ask if he or she wanted to talk. Yet I have also been that person who needed that email, who wanted that insightful and loving intervention, who needed somebody to show me grace without my daring to ask for it.

Ignoring that stream of doubts, I mustered up a little bit of courage and headed out the door into the humid night with a heaping container of vegetable stir-fry, mango, and rice for the guard. It was a simple meal, and I felt ashamed at how much I'd overthought such a small gesture when I shyly gave it to the guard, stumbling over the few Khmer words I knew.

But as I discovered a few nights later, one of my Khmer-speaking co-workers—who was friends with the guard—informed me that this small deed had had more impact than I thought. My co-worker explained that the guard hadn't had any money for food that night. The guard had been wondering how long the pangs of hunger would last when suddenly a plate of home-cooked food—albeit vegetarian food—had showed up at his door.

Choosing mercy and justice in every circumstance is intensely vulnerable. It opens us up to criticism, exposes us to the possibility of our help being rejected, and makes us more susceptible to failure. Moving past paralysis by analysis means we're bound to fail gloriously and embarrass ourselves royally at some point. We're going to think we've brought an innovative solution to a community that ends up being used literally for trash. No matter how many years we've been involved, we're not always going to do it perfectly.

Beyond the setbacks, doubts, fear of failure, and obsessive scrutiny, justice has only ever been sought by imperfect people who keep moving forward.

Misinformed Helping

About a year after my learning experience in Cambodia with the guard, I was walking down a back alley on a brisk mid-October morning in Winnipeg on my way to a coffee shop when I realized I wasn't alone. A few strides ahead of me, carrying three black garbage bags clanking noisily together, a man in well-worn sweatpants and an old, patched jacket was sifting through the industrial-sized metal garbage and recycling bins. My heart broke seeing the face of hunger, homelessness, and desperation standing a few doors down from my own apartment.

Patting myself on the back for having recently grown out of my paralysis-by-analysis phase, I decided to reach out. I always carried a small supply of granola bars in my bag for exactly this purpose. So, I gently approached the man without trying to startle him and greeted him with a smile and a warm hello. Pausing his search through discarded pizza boxes and takeout containers, he looked at me quizzically and returned the greeting.

"You know, I have an extra granola bar with me. Is it all right if I give it to you?" I asked him smilingly.

It took a moment for a small grin to creep across his face, but he politely turned down my offer. Suppressing my surprise, I insisted, without trying to shove charity in his face, that I was happy to share a granola bar. Once again, he smiled and said, "That's all right, ma'am, but I'm not hungry … I'm actually just picking up some recyclables for my company's annual fundraiser for the children's hospital."

My face turned several shades of red. I felt as embarrassed as if I'd asked a pregnant woman when she was due only to find out she wasn't pregnant at all.

The tug-of-war is unending. On the one hand, we're encouraged to always reach out by activists like Dietrich Bonhoeffer, who argued that "silence in the face of evil is evil itself." On the other hand, we're cautioned to be wary of who and how we help. Robert D. Lupton, author of *Toxic Charity*, suggests that we disempower and even destroy people when we try to help them do things they can do for themselves.[2]

Which is better? Which is worse? Do we silence ourselves when we fear we might do more harm than good, or do we risk looking like fools when we reach out to someone who may or may not need or benefit from our help?

Maybe it's neither. Maybe it's not about which is better or worse but which is wiser. It may be more enticing to embark on a high school mission trip to build a school in West Africa, but perhaps it's wiser to hire local builders and purchase local resources to build the school. It may seem more comfortable to ignore somebody asking for help, but perhaps it's the just thing to do—to help if we have the capacity to do so.

Learning to live out a lifestyle of seeking justice, loving mercy, and walking humbly is a long journey. It takes a lot of troubleshooting. It means occasionally making mistakes by trying to help people who don't need our help while bypassing the people that do.

The shame and embarrassment of making a mistake isn't a sign to give up, though. It's not about doing nothing because we fear we will fail or cause harm or waste our time. I'd say it's more about using our lessons learned—both good and bad—to serve more wisely and effectively in the future. It takes practice. It's a process of learning, and every day is an opportunity to find new ways of living a just life.

When Faith Defeats Paralysis by Analysis

There's another reason why paralysis by analysis is such an easy trap to fall into. I think it's the fear of the unknown: the kind of unknown where we might never know the result of our actions.

I have a friend who loves taking risks—the calculated kind. He's the kind of guy who doesn't bat an eye at the thought of skydiving or traveling to obscure countries or starting up his own non-profit. But when it comes to love, he balks. He would rather jump from a plane at 12,500 feet above ground level than take the risk of initiating or accepting a date. And I know why: it's because he knows there's a 99.9 percent chance he will land on the ground and survive the fall, but there are absolutely no guarantees when it comes to romantic relationships.

A lot of us try to avoid risk at all costs—not because we worry the outcome will be bad, but because we have no idea what will happen at all. It's the infinite constellation of possibilities that terrify us into a standstill. So, we don't want to fall in love because we don't know how our vulnerability will be received. We don't want to apply for a new job because we fear the deafening silence of the four-to-six week waiting period before hearing a response from the employer. We don't want to a move to a new city—no matter how exciting the opportunity seems—because we have no clue how the transition would turn out. The uncertainty is gut-wrenching.

And so it is the same with justice—except that we don't always have a four-to-six week waiting period to discover the outcome. Sometimes, we don't ever find out if the help we gave was productive, harmful, or benign. We work with clients we never hear from again. We invest in troubled youth who disappear from our system once they turn eighteen. We pour our hearts and souls into projects even though we don't know with certainty what they'll look like in ten years.

Uncertainty, however, is not an excuse for idleness. We need to become comfortable with the discomfort of not knowing all the answers. We're not God, after all. All we can do is try.

Seeking justice is a prophetic enterprise—and that means we need to do unpopular, even bizarre things at times. Trust me, I've been there. I've had to put myself out on the line and look like a bumbling fool as I try to follow the enigmatic directions that my moral compass sends me.

That so happened last summer during the hottest part of July, when my boyfriend and I noticed a young man sitting in a rusting old car that had far outdriven its life expectancy parked in the open field beside my boyfriend's apartment. Initially, we brushed it off. It was Canada Day weekend, after all, so we figured he was a rebellious young man getting caught up in teenage melodrama and underage drinking with friends out in the field.

Something about it started feeling off when we saw the same car parked there the next day, and the day after that. On the third or fourth day, I decided to investigate. With a peanut butter sandwich and fruit in one hand and my cell phone pre-set to dial an emergency number in the other hand, I approached the young man and his cloud of cigarette smoke to introduce myself. After chatting with him for a few minutes, I found out his name was Dale* and that he'd driven all the way from the West Coast for a construction job that turned out to be exploitative. Graciously but with a hint of embarrassment, he accepted my offerings of food on and went on to share a bit of his story. He told me how his parents had thrown him out when he was thirteen and how he had spent part of his teenage years in prison rather than in school. Aside from a pack of cigarettes and a few changes of clothes in the trunk of his car, Dale had nothing.

I started visiting Dale every day the rest of that week. I'd bring him a bottle of water and a healthy snack, sometimes a phone number for a shelter or an employment service. But mostly we talked. On one of my last visits, he told me he'd been offered a job in construction with a company out of town and that he'd be leaving as soon as he could come up with the gas money for the four-hour drive.

---

*   Note: Name has been changed.

Usually, I have a personal rule against giving money to someone I don't know. I'd rather buy that person a meal or groceries rather than give them cash. But this time I had to make an exception. Sure, Dale could use a nutritious, well-balanced meal from some benevolent strangers, but what he needed even more was the cash to get himself some fuel in order to drive four hours to the town of his job offer.

A hundred dollars doesn't seem like much until you give it to a stranger. And when I gave it to Dale in the form of cash and a gift card for gas, I was immediately flooded by second thoughts and apprehension. Maybe he would take off, burn the money on cigarettes and gambling, and I'd never hear from him again, but my gut instinct told me he was a hard worker and just needed somebody to give him a chance.

The anxiety of not knowing if Dale would use my gift to get to his job site ate away at me for weeks. I thought I needed answers. What I really needed was faith.

Justice and faith are natural companions. Sometimes, I need to trust that my meager sacrifices, my limited resources, and my flawed leadership can be useful and impacting. Sometimes, I need to believe that God can multiply my offerings or use them in unexpected or even grand ways. I think that's exactly what God does: God takes the little we have to give and turns it into something disproportionately profound, something extraordinary and beautiful.

A few weeks after I'd finally let go and accepted my lack of control in Dale's situation, my boyfriend and I received a phone call from the man who had offered Dale the construction job.

Nervously, we asked if Dale was still around or if he had made it to the job site in the first place.

"Dale?" the employer gave a guttural laugh and said something that gave me goose bumps that lasted for days: "Oh, he made it to the site all right. He's the best worker I've ever had."

---

[1]   Simon Romero, "Quinoa's Global Success Creates Quandary at Home," New York Times, March 19, 2011, http://www.nytimes.com/2011/03/20/world/americas/20bolivia.html?_r=1&.

[2]   Robert D. Lupton, Toxic Charity: How the Church Hurts Those They Help and How to Reverse It (New York: HarperCollins, 2011).

CHAPTER 7

Authentic Humanitarianism: What Seeking Justice Really Looks Like

O Divine Master,
Grant that I may not so much seek
To be consoled, as to console;
To be understood, as to understand;
To be loved as to love.
—St. Francis of Assisi

When I stepped off the bus and onto the sandy terrain of the Mexican desert for the first time, I was hit by the startling feeling of coming home. Although I'd never even heard of this town or even set foot in Mexico before, my intuition told me that, here, life was going to start to make sense.

Logically, it shouldn't have seemed that way. Four years of pursuing a degree in justice studies shouldn't have culminated in teaching beginner art courses to twenty children with special needs—but it did. Tens of thousands of dollars spent in tuition fees shouldn't have brought me to working as a volunteer in an agrarian town in the middle of the desert in rural Mexico—but it did. And somehow, it felt strangely right.

Within my first few weeks, I was enraptured. I became immediately captivated by hearing a language spoken so beautifully it didn't even matter I had no idea what was being said. I was enchanted by all my surroundings: by the burning sun rising over the red rock mountains every morning; by the medley of trees covering the mission grounds that harvested macadamia nuts, guava, olives, and oranges; by salsa so strong and spicy that even being in the same room as it made me cough; even by the slight tremors I felt at night from distant earthquakes.

Life in rural Mexico was far from glamorous. As a full-time volunteer, I didn't exactly have a disposable income to burn on after-work outings or on clothes purchased from somewhere more sophisticated than the flea market. Usually I ate three meals of rice per day—yes, even for breakfast—except for the rare occasion my friends and I would pool a few pesos together and "splurge" on flour tortillas and cheese to make quesadillas for dinner.

Still, I found creative ways to thrive—or, at minimum, to make the most of my humble situation. I tried to transform my twenty-foot trailer into a cozy home, starting with hanging mismatched bed sheets as curtains and adorning my walls with crafts my students had made for me. I asked one of the maintenance staff to dislodge a mushroom growing out of my wall and opted to spruce up the patch of sand and dirt outside my trailer. A friend attempted to help create an aesthetically pleasing lawn for me by transplanting the stem of a cactus next to my doorstep and triumphantly declared it to be an unparalleled work of brilliant landscaping.

My simple lifestyle suited me unmistakably, but my purpose—and the impact of it—was less clear. At first, I struggled to connect my work to a greater vision of social justice, especially with all the sensationalized assumptions and preconceived notions I had of international humanitarian service. There was nothing extraordinary, nothing noble about what I was doing. While my former classmates were padding their resumés and lining their wallets from prestigious government jobs, I was wiping runny noses between desperate attempts to find clever ways of repurposing toilet paper rolls and discarded magazines for art projects.

Whisked away from the regimented order of my scholarly domain at university, I felt far outside my comfort zone being plunged into a chaotic environment of glue sticks and fingerpaint. Perhaps the biggest irony of teaching kids with special needs in Latin America was the fact I had no training in teaching or child care or special needs, no dexterity in Spanish, and no previous desire to travel to Mexico whatsoever—let alone live there. Four years of social justice training hadn't exactly included any tutorials on efficient diaper-changing methods for hyperactive children. We hadn't learned any techniques on how to safely manoeuvre a toothbrush for a child who was born with an extra set of teeth that she used as a lethal weapon. I was underprepared, overwhelmed, and incalculably confused about how this role fit into my ten-year plan.

Every day, I felt bound by a question I didn't know the answer to: *Am I really making a difference?*

When Our Hands Are Tied

Like most people, I grew up with a far-fetched version of what it meant to seek justice. Church and my faith community tended to imply that justice meant short-term mission trips to Honduras or Haiti—which, to me, always seemed more like a really holy-sounding vacation. School told me it meant eradicating apartheid like Nelson Mandela or rescuing enslaved families like Harriet Tubman. Hollywood films told me it meant crime-fighting secret service, where the good guys always win.

No matter what the source, humanitarianism seems to be defined by extremes. Sometimes it's constructed more as an adventure to scratch off a bucket list. It's holding cute babies with dirt-smudged faces as the perfect accessory for photos to send home. It's getting a nice tan over spring break while helping to build a school in Tanzania.

Or its execution is strongly exaggerated. It's expected to come with a reckless bravado that's unsafe, unwise, and unrealistic. It's being canonized as a hero for bringing solar-power technology to hundreds of villages or leading undercover raids to unshackle trafficked Eastern European women from chains inside a brothel in a cosmopolitan city.

And there's a big problem with that: when seeking justice is sensationalized, nobody prepares you for the grit.

At the outset of my training, nobody talked to me about burnout. Nobody mentioned the high rates of depression and anxiety among humanitarians. Nobody told me that as many as 30 percent of aid workers suffer from symptoms of post-traumatic stress disorder.[1] It took my own experience of these things to find that out the hard way.

When seeking justice is glamorized, the ordinary quests aren't validated. It only seems to count if service is overseas or in an unsafe and hostile environment. Most of all, you've got to be somewhere close to saintly in order to be a bona fide justice seeker—and that just isn't true.

Yet all of the human icons of justice that I heralded as a child were people like Rosa Parks, whose refusal to give up her seat on a city bus made huge legislative impact. Or Laura Secord, who trekked thirty-two kilometres by foot to warn British soldiers of an impending military attack. I grew up revering Martin Luther King Jr. and how he inspired an entire race of people to become active participants in a non-violent campaign for justice.

All my humanitarian role models are people I deeply respect but can't replicate. They were all given medals and awarded Nobel Peace Prizes and have had statues enshrined in their honour—and for good reason. But when I measure myself against people like these, I'm dwarfed by them. Any effort I make seems inconsequential and irrelevant in comparison. They may have been ordinary people, but they did extraordinary things that just aren't in my capacity to do, because no matter the cause, I don't think I could ever be bold enough to cause a public disturbance on the transit system. As passionate as I am about racial equality, I don't expect to be the kind of orator who can deliver the next "I Have a Dream" speech to a quarter of a million people.

But that's exactly what happens when we sensationalize humanitarianism. When seeking justice is constructed around status, it separates the moral elite from the rest of us who can only read about their legacies in the news while knowing we could never aspire to such greatness. It means justice is a badge of honour only to be worn by the Joan of Arcs and Gandhis of the world. It's glorified and even hyperbolized to make us feel as if there is only a certain type of person with predetermined qualifications who can be knighted as a seeker of justice.

In the midst of all this triumphalism, non-profits are losing their focus. Seldom do they spotlight their efforts to build communities through forging relationships rooted in love, compassion, and respect as their essence and core anymore. Because, quite frankly, love fails to translate quantifiably into a grant application or a compelling infographic or a trendy fundraising campaign. The simple things aren't enough anymore. We demand the grandiose.

That's the other problem. On a public scale, justice is supposed to be sought in a way that produces outcomes that often outpace what humanitarians can plausibly provide. Donors have big expectations: they want to see us eradicate racism or end human trafficking, as if these were basic items to scratch off a to-do list. Once, I had the challenge of working with a major funder who was convinced that teaching communication skills in twenty rural villages would reduce divorce rates at the provincial level within one year. By trying to meet such unrealistic and—quite frankly, ridiculous—benchmarks, we set ourselves up for failure.

And so, instead of working together, non-profits have to compete in a winner-takes-all race for funding. The more complicated the indicators, the more sophisticated the outreach strategies, the more flashy the proposal, then the more likely the project will be funded. No longer is working to protect a child's happiness or safety enough—it needs to be more complicated than that.

How do we seek justice when our hands our tied? How do we overcome the power imbalance of the traditional non-profit model where we write proposals based on what we *think* a donor wants to fund? How effective is spending the majority of our time trying to please the funding agency than actually working with the people we're supposed to be helping?

Perhaps one of the reasons why organizations fabricate their statistics and sensationalize their stories is because they're buckling under all this pressure of needing to reach certain quotas based on their funding agreements. Somehow they must keep donors interested and impressed—and the truth is no longer enough. It's not an excuse; it doesn't justify the dishonesty. But it does shed some light on why non-profits feel they have to embellish their work in the first place.

Maybe it's time for a new kind of humanitarianism. The kind that's authentic. The kind that sees justice in the small and mundane efforts. The kind that lets humanitarians be humans.

A New Kind of Humanitarianism

Teaching art classes to kids in Mexico didn't exactly make me feel like Canada's version of Malala Yousafzai. Most days, I just felt like a mess. Helping a nine-year-old boy with cerebral palsy to drag his paintbrush across a blank page or washing the soiled clothes of my six-year-old sidekick with Down's syndrome seemed immaterial and insignificant.

Sure, the work was an enjoyable challenge. The only thing that was more limited than our meagre supply closet of pipe cleaners and popsicle sticks was my total lack of translatable skills or experience. Everything was further complicated by trying to accommodate the vast scope of different learning abilities of my students. Each one of my art classes was a frenzy of rushing from desk to desk, helping one student with muscular dystrophy to reach for his scissors, and then swooping over to a student with ADHD to ensure he didn't accidentally plunge his scissors into his body.

No, spending my days covered in dirt and sweat wasn't exactly how I'd pictured myself as a recent university graduate. Making low-budget crafts in a classroom full of Spanish-speaking children was a capacity I'd never imagined I'd work in. And yet those few months I spent living out of a trailer in the middle of the desert turned out to be one of the most pivotal seasons of my life—mainly because of Julia.

On my first day on the job, my supervisor told me I'd be assigned to one child to vigilantly monitor at all times. She pointed me toward a tiny girl with Down's syndrome sitting in a high chair, her face smeared with porridge while wearing a mischievous grin. With virtually no instruction, my supervisor told me her name was Julia and sternly warned me, "Watch out, she has really bad diarrhea."

Before the end of my first day, I was mentally comparing the fee of changing my flight several months down the road with the emotional cost of staying in Mexico. I needed to get out of there as soon as possible. Justice couldn't possibly be served with a mop and a bucket to clean up excrement on the floor.

There was no way that hand puppets and papier mâché crafts were a meaningful contribution to the humanitarian agenda.

Contempt began consuming me as the practical route my peers had taken seemed sickeningly appealing to me. Why hadn't I more seriously entertained thoughts of working with a governmental advocacy agency or applying to Ivy League graduate studies instead? What kind of value could possibly become of such a bizarre experience as this? As I hacked away at every possible explanation and examined every escape route, a completely unheralded development came to be: Julia stole my heart.

Even I, the resolute academic with the ten-year life plan who was anything but a kid person, started to love this six-year-old child with a fierceness I couldn't explain. The resentfulness I once felt toward my workweek reversed into resentfulness toward the weekends, because they meant I had to agonize until Monday before I could see Julia again. I taught her how to ride a bicycle, and she taught me how it was possible to love somebody else's daughter as if she were my own.

Did the little I have to offer count as justice sought? Can we call it "doing justice" when we're not dressed in a suit in the middle of a courtroom but are untrained teachers wearing thrift-store clothing in the middle of the desert? Does it count for something when, instead of riding in on a white horse to save the whole village, we're just doing the best we can to love one small child?

Maybe even the smallest gestures of love and kindness count for something. Maybe my art classes went beyond the act of teaching and were a form of physical therapy, especially for the students with spina bifida and cerebral palsy. Maybe teaching art was more than a fun way to playfully interact with my students and was about investing steadfast love and consistent care in each of them—something they severely lacked at home. Maybe it wasn't just about art but about creating the opportunity for the underdogs in math and language classes to build confidence and shine in a way they'd never experienced.

And maybe Julia was only one child, and I was only one teacher. But perhaps the bond I forged with her as her teacher and caregiver was rooted in the sort of love that felt more powerful than an impact report could convey.

Maybe the outcomes that the world expects to see are what justice harvests, but the relationships are where justice is planted. For me in Mexico, seeking justice was less about intrepid aspirations and more about helping to plant seeds. Seeds of love and hope and self-esteem. Seeds that would hopefully come to flourish in potentially profound ways long after I was gone.

What Seeking Justice Really Looks Like

My own journey of learning to fight against human trafficking didn't exactly look like a scene with Liam Neeson in the blockbuster film *Taken*. I didn't strap on my combat boots every day to bust down brothel doors under the cover of darkness or parachute myself into villages to pull children out of garment factories. Oftentimes, managing projects that intervened in human trafficking looked like the dull grind of administrative work in a dimly lit office without any windows until the wee hours of the following morning.

For me at the outset, the battle against human trafficking meant spending a lot of time drafting dozens of spreadsheets with lists of desired outcomes and indicators of meeting those outcomes. Instead of having fistfights with traffickers, I was waging email wars to find people with copious amounts of money who were willing to fund our counter-trafficking projects. I celebrated our victories by typing out lengthy progress reports with quantitative data that, frustratingly enough, didn't accurately represent the transformational change we were aiming to create in communities.

Given the scope of the projects I had to manage, many late-night conference calls ensued until well past two in the morning. Soon enough, I was working upwards of fourteen hours a day, seven days a week, without a thought of what life might be like to have an occasional weekend or evening off.

Glamorizing human trafficking is counterproductive and unhelpful: it turns real-life nightmares into entertainment, manufactures a false understanding of the plight of victims, and further confuses the general public on how to respond. It's unethical: it perpetuates another form of exploitation by embellishing the stories of trafficking survivors. And it's unfair for social justice workers: it twists our stories to make our work sound exciting and adventurous while ignoring the true costs of the work—the secondary traumas, the compassion fatigue, the lost hope, and burnout.

What humanitarians do every day isn't what you think. What makes it so hard isn't always what you expect. Of course, the work and its inherent traumas can be fatiguing. But sometimes what's most difficult is the lifestyle itself.

It's being too drained in the evening to go out with friends. It's feeling constantly estranged from regular conversations because you haven't had the time to keep up with the celebrity gossip or the latest Hollywood hit at the box office. It's falling into a habit of using your boyfriend or girlfriend or spouse as an untrained counsellor to off-load your problems onto and expecting way too much from them. It's the exhaustion of having the justice advocate button permanently switched on: always speaking cautiously and politically correctly, always setting an example for friends by buying the ethically-sourced option, always being prepared to speak on behalf of every humanitarian that ever lived.

For justice workers living overseas, sometimes the most tiresome thing isn't the work itself but is the acclimating to a new culture. It's having a hard time stomaching the food or trying to learn a language that throws out every rule learned in elementary phonics classes. Sometimes what's hard is dealing with the minor stresses of foreign housing: the daily battles with rodents and insects, the walls so thin that the snoring of your neighbour keeps you up all night, or the loud chanting from the temple next door that wakes you up at three-thirty every morning. For me, it was how strongly my malaria medication affected my mood and sleeping habits, rendering me comatose from the time I left work in the evening until the following morning. How do you connect with a culture or make new friends when you can barely stay awake? What kind of life consists exclusively of working and sleeping and working and sleeping?

Overall, my own experience doesn't measure up to the popularized idea of what it takes to seek justice. One day seeking justice to me meant washing out the bloodstained dress of a seventeen-year-old girl who told me the story of how it came to be tarnished. Sitting on the floor of my office, I gently scrubbed her new dress from a makeshift laundry tub—a Rubbermaid container that had stored some of my files—while she bravely tried to downplay the severity of the domestic abuse from which she had narrowly escaped. A blockbuster film might've portrayed me physically intervening before her drunken mother brought down the hammer one more time on her teenage daughter. But my experience of seeking justice has never worked like that. Sometimes it comes humbly and soft-spoken in the little moments.

To me, justice looks like being caked in layers of mud while trying to get a quad unstuck to deliver tree seedlings to a crew of ambitious young twenty-year-olds reforesting a block of logged land. It looks like sleeping with one eye open in shady low-budget hotels with kicked-in door locks while on a state-wide tour to raise meagre charitable funds at speaking events for bored crowds of teenagers. It looks like staying up until four in the morning to madly finish writing project proposals, under the pressure of knowing the quality of this proposal will ultimately decide whether or not a donor will fund valuable community-based programming.

Justice looks like doing the work that nobody else wants to do because unclogging toilets or folding newsletters or stacking chairs doesn't feel much like seeking justice.

It looks like trying to oversee a smelly, hot bus full of children from low-income families who neither have bladder control nor access to showers. It looks like an unpaid volunteer armed with rubber gloves and a bucket, inhaling fresh air before he disappears into the boys' bathroom at a school for kids with special needs. It looks like a twenty-five-year-old manager of an inner-city feeding program cleaning out mouldy food from the fridge with grime up to her elbows. It looks like dragging a garbage bag full of diapers, used birth-control devices, discarded needles, and other trash through an inner-city neighbourhood in order to help improve its safety and image.

It's finding ways to thrive even with the limits of a non-profit salary and time restrictions. It's trying to creatively disguise second-hand clothes as business-casual attire at fundraising events we'd rather not attend. It's saving up vacation time simply to spend a reclusive week locked up at home, sleeping off months of eighty-hour weeks. It's eating instant noodles like a starving university student on a strict budget with whatever dignity is left.

At times, I've felt ashamed to tell my story of what I *really* do, because it doesn't match the expectations of the idealized humanitarian. I don't save women from the streets or smuggle children out of sweatshops. I don't live somewhere out in the jungle, rescuing child soldiers under the cover of darkness. And when I started realizing and accepting that justice hasn't looked at all like a scene from a James Bond film, I wondered if my friends and colleagues in similar social justice roles felt the same way. Turns out most of them do.

Opening the floodgates for honest dialogue causes all sorts of stories of solidarity to come gushing out. A former co-worker, who is the managing director of a job-training centre for survivors of human trafficking, admits she has days of spending more time fixing a clogged grease trap in the kitchen than teaching survivors cooking skills. My friend in Southeast Asia often spends hours pushing her motorbike through knee-deep mud in monsoon season to reach a hot, one-room schoolhouse, where she teaches teenagers how to use computers and make jewellery to sell. A former boss of mine who participated in typhoon-relief efforts was once drenched in manure sprayed from a water buffalo while loading up sandbags and ended up catching a tropical virus that rendered her sick for weeks.

For my friend in Lebanon, her work with Syrian refugees looks more like sixteen-hour days spent in UN conference rooms. There's my friend who spent Christmas alone in his trailer in Latin America because he'd committed to taking care of a resource-poor local family over the holiday season. I know plenty of friends who pick up shifts at fast-food joints or drive commercial vehicles at night for office-supply companies because the non-profit organization they work for can't pay them enough to support their families. But somehow, they manage. Because when it comes to something you believe to be right, it doesn't matter how foolish you look or dull the work might be—it's worth it.

Planting Trees We Never Sit Under

For years, I've been on a relentless crusade to find an adequate definition of justice—not so much for the purpose of semantics as to try to understand the thing that was the core of my human existence and purpose. The ancient Greek philosophers had a lot to say about defining justice, as did my university professors. Outside academia, I heard it spoken about in punitive terms as law enforcement or as something we "get" when we've been wronged—almost like something we can pick up in a packaged box from a shelf at the supermarket. Other times, the definition of justice changed depending on which side of the political spectrum you were on: pro-life or pro-choice, anti-immigration or open borders, homophobic or gay inclusive, pro-war or pacifism. It was all completely subjective.

My own experience of justice doesn't look like a paint-by-numbers sort of project. It has never come neatly packaged in the literal ask-and-you-shall-receive model. Above all else, justice has never brought about the surplus of rewards and immediate satisfaction that those outside the non-profit world seem to think we get. Seeking justice has never looked like a victory lap or a knighting ceremony—and it sure doesn't feel like one either.

In my life, justice is not just stitching together a ripped seam but also having a knotted ball of thread unravelling in my hands, not knowing where else to start—except to make myself start somewhere. Not just holding adorable, underprivileged children in my arms but also wiping the runny noses of kids I don't even know, washing their hair and their stained clothes, and crossing my fingers that I won't get lice or bedbugs. Not just the "rewarding" feelings from being the educator, the leader, the comforter—but also, most of the time, feeling like *I'm* the one who needs to be taught, who needs to listen, who needs to be comforted.

Seeking justice isn't about nobility. It's about serving with authenticity, integrity, and honour. It's modest and sometimes even unnoticed. It's the kind of humble service Mother Teresa once talked about—the kind that "plants some trees we never sit under."

It's as simple and as complicated as love: terribly messy yet indescribably beautiful too. And when the glitter has fallen, the strobe lights are unplugged, and all the glamorized nonsense is stripped away, seeking justice looks more and more like imperfect people who are comfortable enough with doing a lot of work without the glory.

---

[1] Rich McEchran, "Aid Workers and Post-traumatic Stress Disorder," Guardian, March 3, 2014, http://www.theguardian.com/global-development-professionals-network/2014/mar/03/post-traumantic-stress-disorder-aid-workers.

PART II

LIVING WELL

There are those who seek knowledge
for the sake of knowledge; that is curiosity.
There are those who seek knowledge
to be known by others; that is vanity.
There are those who seek knowledge
in order to serve; that is love.
—Bernard of Clairvaux

CHAPTER 8

Dehumanized Humanitarians: The Problem with Being a Martyr

> If people knew how hard I worked to get my
> mastery, it wouldn't seem so wonderful at all.
> —Michelangelo

Cruising steadily through fog and fragmented memories, I guided my rental car farther into the foothills of the Rocky Mountains with an ominous feeling about all the uncertainties before me. With every kilometre, I travelled deeper into unknown territory, farther from home, and closer to a crippling discovery I'd needed to learn for years.

Along the drive, the parting words people had said to me before I'd left home slowly meandered through my mind. All were words of good intentions from former university professors and church members, distant relatives, and close friends. Yet all were words predicated on misconstrued conclusions about the honourability of this justice endeavour I was embarking on, which I already felt inadequate for.

Assuming my work was inextricably connected to morality and character, these well-meaning words hinted at the common perception that my vocational aspirations placed me in a different category of human. That I was somehow poised to dwell outside the realm of regular fears and flaws and failures. That honour and heroism were directly connected to being a humanitarian.

At least, that's what they thought. Little did anyone know—anyone including myself—that this journey for justice was about to introduce an entirely new experience of honour.

"It Sounds Like You're Going to Be Doing Very Noble Work Where You're Heading."

The farther I drove, the more these kinds of words haunted me. My whole body felt sluggish, weighed down by the burden of being consecrated with everyone's subtle demands of superhumanity from me. Barely had I begun this journey, and already I felt discouraged by it.

Other people set unrealistic expectations for my coworkers and me as humanitarians—expectations that we didn't necessarily hold for ourselves. It created a double standard: most people realize their limitations disqualify them from the unattainable realm of nobility and perfection, yet these same qualities are expected of humanitarians and their organizations, setting them up for failure.

Gradually the road signs started indicating I had almost reached the first destination along my way. I didn't know what was about to unfold. And yet, with the weight of bitterness and unattainable expectations brewing beneath, I suspected that *something* would.

"I Admire You for Being So Strong. You're Brave for Leaving All Your Family and Friends Behind."

By the time I started slowing down to find the hotel I'd be staying in for the next two weeks, it started to occur to me that perhaps this external expectation of ironclad perfection and perseverance wasn't the kind of strength I wanted to aspire to have anymore.

Once I'd checked in, I dragged the suitcase I'd be living out of for the next six months to my hotel room. My suite, while spacious and adorned in the regality of fine linens and elegant drapes, felt nevertheless empty and impersonal to me. Shivering from the damp cold and the weariness of my trip, I listened to the sound of silence for a few disconcerting moments before unpacking some of the contents of my suitcase to bring some remnants of home and familiarity into the room.

I was only twenty-three at the time, but I could already feel the aches of loneliness of somebody with decades more years of life than I. Already I felt haunted by the loss of too many moments I would never get to experience. The loss of not being able to attend family reunions and graduation ceremonies. The loss of not being around during the year of my sister's engagement or my college roommate's wedding. The loss of missing out on holding the newborn babies of friends I hadn't seen for years.

Of course, I had made my own set of memories in the meantime. But the nature of my overseas work meant that few of these memories included the people I loved most.

Standing in the middle of my suite, I felt exhausted from the drive—and even more exhausted from mourning the memories that would only ever belong to others and never to me. Too cowardly to allow myself to feel the pangs of loneliness, I grabbed the keys of my rental car and left behind the empty hotel room to escape its dull silence.

Pulling out the directions to my organization's headquarters, I decided to scope out its location before the early-morning orientation session the next day. I needed to distract myself from obsessively lingering on the past and redirect myself to focus on the present moment. I was suffocating.

"Working for a Humanitarian Organization Must Mean You Feel Like You're Making Such a Difference!"

It wasn't the magnitude that shocked me as much as the opulence. Gazing across the campus—at the intricate stonework, the grandeur of floor-to-ceiling windows, the immaculate gardens—I wondered if my navigational skills had failed me.

They hadn't.

Being part of a major international relief and development organization, I thought we were resistant to the entanglement of consumer-driven greed and materialistic desires. I thought we fell outside the norm of being defined by social status and paycheques. I thought we didn't care about the salaries we earned or the cars we drove or the square footage of the buildings we worked in. But the moment I arrived on campus, I couldn't tell if I had stumbled upon the international headquarters of a non-profit poverty-alleviation organization or a multi-billion-dollar corporate resort.

When the orientation sessions began the following morning, my sense of premonition grew. I was distressed by the absence of fair-trade coffee dispensers, the lack of recycling and compost bins, and the amount of blatant wastefulness I saw. Weren't we supposed to live differently? Wasn't a life of seeking justice supposed to permeate every aspect of our lives, including our ethical use of resources? Wasn't there a terrible hypocrisy in printing promotional T-shirts bearing our logo when the materials were made of cotton picked by six-year-olds forced to work in the fields of Uzbekistan? Did anyone else feel uncomfortable with discussing best practices in preventing labour trafficking from lavish boardrooms while serving coffee harvested by children from the Ivory Coast?

During the entire two weeks of training, I found myself struggling between the dichotomy of who we claimed we were and who we actually seemed to be. Initially, I was enraptured by the words the directors used to describe the organization's projects: words like *enrichment* and *transformation* and *renewal*. Words spoken by groomed Caucasian men in neatly pressed suits, who were thoroughly comfortable making powerful claims about their efforts to end child hunger in countries they had never travelled. Words that, after a few days, seemed to be no more than words.

I felt ashamed. Every night, I returned to a king suite at a hotel I could never afford on my own dime. Every morning, I watched baskets of bagels and pots of coffee being tossed from the hotel's buffet line when they sat for longer than an hour or two.

And every day, I sat in a posh conference room during training, listening to two different stories: the one being spoken and the one left unsaid.

Given the confusing disconnect between our projects that addressed poverty overseas and the way in which we were trying to carry out that work, I didn't feel as though we were making a difference at all. I felt no different from anybody else.

"You're Going to Cambodia? That Sounds So Exotic! That's Near Brazil, Right?"

Fortunately, our team of trainees gained respite from the unpalatable lecture series during the next two days of interactive safety training. Through a series of simulations and practical application, we intensively examined the worst-case scenarios we hoped to never experience but were trained to handle: skeptical airport authorities in closed countries, disgruntled government officials, mass protests, even armed kidnappers and militia forces. Halfway through the training, a newlywed couple became so disturbed by the upsetting content of the trainings that they made a quiet exit and returned home.

While most of my colleagues were heading to high-conflict areas, such as South Sudan and Iraq, I was bound for a subtly known developing nation with a dark history and minimal media coverage: Cambodia. While it hadn't made international headlines for civil war since the late 1970s, Cambodia was still nursing its wounds in the wake of the Khmer Rouge genocide that had killed nearly two million people.[1] Over thirty years later, the country was still suffering the endemic post-conflict problems of rampant violence, corruption, lawlessness with impunity, widespread poverty, and a lack of education.

Fuelled by many of the nation's developmental issues, Cambodia has also become a breeding grounds for exploitation. Being a global hotspot as a source, transit, and destination country for human trafficking, Cambodia was in dire need of change—and I, convinced I was invincible, decided to help. Without any warning of how much it would break me, my organization deployed me to research and implement methods of effectively preventing human trafficking in the rural villages of northern Cambodia.

All I knew about Cambodia at the time of my orientation were impersonal facts. I knew the UN classified Cambodia as one of the least developed, most food-deficient, poorest countries in the world.[2] I knew the statistical references: that out of Cambodia's 13.4 million people, about 35 percent live below the poverty line in a state of rampant hunger and malnutrition.[3] I knew it was ranked as a Tier 3 Watch List nation for having one of the world's lowest governmental responses to prevent human trafficking, prosecute traffickers, and protect victims.[4]

What I didn't know was what it would be like to serve in this context and how much my world was about to be turned upside down.

"So How Quickly Did You Become Fluent in the Local Language?"

When I stepped off a double-decker Korean Air jet in Phnom Penh after two weeks of training and forty unpleasant hours of flights and airports, my first experience of Cambodia came in the form of a catatonic wave of humidity. Although my flight landed at midnight, the thermometer was still holding on to an unrelenting forty degrees Celsius. Having departed from Canada in the brutal mid-winter climate of negative forty degrees Celsius, the eighty-degree change in temperature left me in shock.

Over the next few months of attempting to integrate into Cambodian society, the heat alone was enough of a factor in vaporizing any of my energy left over from my work. But even though I had always identified myself as an off-the-charts liberal with enough open-mindedness and flexibility to blend myself adaptively into any foreign circumstance, I was surprised with how much I ended up struggling with culture shock.

Of course, I was able to easily adjust to certain rituals more than others—like learning to bow in the presence of others, eating rice at every meal, or replacing a fork and knife with a pair of chopsticks or a spoon. I loved the communal meals, the intentional way Cambodians created community, and the prioritization of people before productivity in the workplace. I grew to appreciate the sense of humour and ease by which many Cambodians lived and how everyone seemed to have a hammock or straw mat on hand to nap on for a couple of hours during the hottest part of the day.

Yet I felt constantly drained by other elements of the local culture. I had trouble yielding to gendered constructs rendering me "weak" in the eyes of locals as a young woman. I shuddered with every reminder of the old Cambodian proverb "Men are like gold; women are like cloth," which men often used to justify violence against girls and women. I couldn't get used to how corruption permeated almost every level of society, from teachers taking bribes from their students to police officers threatening to kill drivers for payoffs.

For the most part, my integration into the ways of life in Cambodia felt more exhausting than energizing. Even a simple grocery run was a hectic, full-body experience and often validated a post-market recovery nap. Driving to the market meant risking my life on chaotic and unregulated roadways, regardless of whether I was driving a company SUV or a motorbike. The market was loud and hot, lined by men who would stare and catcall at me while puffing on cigarettes and drinking can after can of beer. Usually as the only white woman in the market, I called far more attention and way less bargaining power than I was comfortable with too.

Contrary to the popular belief of having a glamorized international lifestyle, my daily routine was simple, even mundane. I didn't spend all my time outside of work attending colourful religious festivals or being advised by monks dressed in saffron robes or exploring the ancient ruins of Angkor Wat every weekend. Truthfully, out of necessity I preferred to spend my precious yet limited time off to catch up on sleep rather than commit to hours of sitting in a sweltering classroom trying to sound out a tonal language or otherwise becoming an expert in navigating the local culture.

Most of the time, I was too tired to force myself to become integrated into a new culture. All I wanted was survival.

"Were You over There to Teach Them English or What?"

I left my home in Canada committed to a six-month overseas internship where I would conduct research on human trafficking prevention strategies. It wasn't about trying to Westernize the villages we worked in but to consult with them in co-developing culturally appropriate ways of building resilience against labour exploitation.

Deeply passionate about my research, I travelled throughout the country for a couple of months to interview different NGOs and government agencies that had already been engaged for decades in applying sustainable-livelihood approaches to international development. Visiting site after site, I witnessed how creating jobs in villages and supporting business-development pursuits to bolster economic opportunities helped lift the burden of desperation. I hosted focus group discussions in dozens of villages to open the dialogue with the people who had the fewest resources and the greatest susceptibility to being trafficked. After analyzing all the data, I wrote a lengthy report with recommendations on how to build the foundations of a program to strengthen livelihoods and establish viable job opportunities within the Cambodian market.

Even though my living conditions were harsh, I was thrilled to help launch a platform for preventing human trafficking. Finally I had the opportunity to directly address the injustice I'd always felt so strongly called to fight against.

Within a few short weeks, an unsuspecting turn of events halted my zest for this project. After only a couple of months into my internship, my supervisor left Cambodia unexpectedly, creating a state of panic for our directors. Knowing that our counter-trafficking projects were at the precipice of groundbreaking impact in the villages we served, my directors were urgent in their desire to fill the position she had abdicated as soon as possible.

Early on a Saturday morning, even before I was fully caffeinated, one of the directors called me and offered me her two-year job contract. Making persuasive and guilt-inciting comments about "Christian duty" and how much the projects and staff depended on me, my director had nudged me into a corner I didn't think I could escape from.

I was already burned out, disenchanted, and homesick. Yet even though my gut instinct told me otherwise, I accepted the job—without realizing that even humanitarians have the option to say no.

"From the Looks of Those Charitable Gift Catalogues, Humanitarian Organizations Seem to Be Really Well Run!"

It turned out to be one of the worst decisions I've ever made.

At only twenty-three years old, I was overwhelmed enough by the drastic transition from short-term intern to permanent manager. The job was already overwhelming enough with its broad scope of responsibilities, from accounting (right down to calculating an annual 3 percent raise in salary for staff while drafting a $750,000 project budget) to human resources (doing all the hiring, firing, staff discipline, and even counselling of distressed colleagues).

Seeing me as somewhat of a windup toy—easily manipulated, easily unleashed—my supervisors decided against recruiting new staff to coordinate two additional projects in order to cut their budget and save on the time-consuming hiring process. Instead they delegated these projects to the youngest, newest, most inexperienced person in the office: me.

Managing multiple projects far outside my comfort zone and field of expertise was daunting. In order to conquer the steep learning curve, my weekends became consumed by drafting up project proposals and budgets. I found myself researching project materials I knew nothing about: vaccinations for small poultry stock … transportation methods for shipments of five hundred bicycles to be distributed at elementary schools in rural locations with impassable road access … weather-durable materials for chicken coops that would need to survive monsoon season … high-torque trucks that could carry heavy loads of equipment while plowing through knee-deep mud. Somehow I ungracefully morphed into a chicken farmer, veterinarian, engineer, and entrepreneurship advisor, in addition to advocating for the protection of over one hundred villages vulnerable to human trafficking.

Despite the smiling faces of staff representing the one side of our organization on our website, gift catalogues, and newsletters, most of us in the trenches of development work were slowly burning out. Promotional materials didn't convey the shortage of staff, the unmanageable workloads, or the lack of support that was leaving us with anything but smiles. Our stories were buried beneath layers of paperwork and shame.

Maybe it was a reflection of my organization being disorganized or an indication of trying to take on too much. But to me, it was a lack of concern for the well-being of staff who had chosen to leave their families, comfort, and safety to live in solidarity, support, and service of people who thought the world had forgotten about them. The expectation of martyrdom was breeding a disease of burnout, an epidemic of dehumanized humanitarians.

"You've Probably Seen Some Very Broken People with the Work That You Do."

It was almost too late before I realized it wasn't only my clients and wasn't only my staff who were damaged. It took many years of working on other people's problems before I could see how much of a mess *I* was—that I was broken too.

Broken from trauma I'd repressed for years. Broken from unresolved relational conflict. Broken from isolating myself from love I didn't think I deserved. Broken from all the hurt I'd seen and experienced in my work without debriefing. Broken from pushing myself to work harder for too long, in spite of physical injury and emotional pain. Broken from expecting myself to be perfectly unbroken. And broken from feeling I wasn't allowed to feel broken.

I still wanted to be a humanitarian. I still wanted to help. I just didn't want to be anybody's hero anymore.

1   Dan Fletcher, "A Brief History of the Khmer Rouge," Time, February 17, 2009, http://content.time.com/time/world/article/0,8599,1879785,00.html.

2   UNDP, Cambodia Human Development Report 2007: Expanding Choices for Rural People, http://hdr.undp.org/en/reports/national/asiathepacific/cambodia/Cambodia_HDR_2007.pdf(Accessed May 5, 2013).

3   Central Intelligence Agency, The CIA World Factbook 2010 (New York: Skyhorse Publishing), 2009.

4   US Department of State, Trafficking in Persons Report 2012 (June 2012), http://www.state.gov/j/tip/rls/tiprpt/2012/.

CHAPTER 9

Love within Limits:
Doing the Best We Can

Do not think that love, in order to be
genuine, has to be extraordinary.
What we need is to love without getting tired.
—Mother Teresa

It was midday, but we weren't even close to being halfway through our hike. Threatening storm clouds—the regalia of monsoon season—began inching their way closer and closer in a defensive swirl of impending doom as we impatiently waited for the last member of our trekking group to catch up.

I was in the mountains of Northern Thailand, trying to rest and regroup on a week-long break from my work in rural Cambodia. Of course, resting isn't much of a skill of mine, so by the second day of my "vacation," I found myself riding in the back of a *songthaew*—a Thai pickup truck that serves as a passenger vehicle for public transit—on my way for a rigorous jungle hike.

We had hardly covered a few kilometres of breathtaking scenery on foot before the delays began. While our group was comprised almost entirely of fit, overzealous twentysomethings, there was one woman nearing retirement age who was lagging far behind. Although her gumption was admirable, she was still recovering from a particularly nasty case of strep throat, which would have made the hike nearly impossible for anyone to tackle.

As we waited, the expressions on our faces progressed from bemused to irritated to stone-cold bitter as we paused at half-hour intervals to wait for her. Gradually, I allowed the setbacks to grate away at my attitude too: Why hadn't she evaluated her condition a little more wisely and stayed in bed today? What was she hoping to gain from pushing her limits this far? Why can't she just let go of whatever she needs to prove?

It wasn't until we stumbled back to our *songthaew* in a haze of twilight at the end of the arduous climb—much later than expected—that I discovered my irritation was derived from within, not without. Begrudgingly, I realized just how much I could relate to this woman's attitude of invincibility. I was deeply familiar with that compulsive need to push myself harder and that inability to release my need for control and let go of my pride. I knew exactly what it was like trying to draw a heavy curtain reflecting an illusion of infinite strength when, behind the scenes, I was doubled over in pain. Too ashamed to admit I was struggling, too proud to accept my limits.

Pushing the Limit

Those of us who live a self-perpetuating legacy of perfectionism try to outrun vulnerability at all costs. We'll try to fool everyone around us that we can handle more than our share, even when we're running on empty. But that doesn't work for long. Sooner or later, the myth of self-sufficiency falls apart on us. Sooner or later, we're confronted by the stark but humbling reality that we were created with limits—not to demoralize or incapacitate us but to turn us toward the One who created us.

I've spent a good portion of my life ignoring my own limits across all spectrums: physical, mental, relational, emotional, spiritual. More than once in my lifetime, I've been willing to sacrifice my personal health in order to appear competent. I shudder while remembering my second summer as a tree planter in the wilderness of northern British Columbia when I tried to tackle my first full day of planting with a dangerous amount of gusto that led to a severe injury in my right knee—by lunchtime. As if I had something to prove, I pushed myself even more vigorously the next day instead of easing up and threw out my left knee too.

When my foreman found out through a fellow tree planter that I had injured both knees, he sent me to a doctor, who proceeded to tell me I would probably never run again, let alone continue planting trees that summer.

My brand of perfectionism couldn't accept being told "you can't." So, being the type who thrives on ambitious challenges, I ignored my doctor's note, bought a couple of knee braces, and stocked up on ibuprofen. After one day off work to "recover," I was back loading boxes of trees into our truck at five thirty the following morning, trying to show my tree-planting crew how resilient I was.

That summer wasn't the first time I'd deceived myself into thinking I was engaged in some noble cause when it was more about my inability to let go of stubborn adherence to the doctrine of self-sufficiency. It wasn't until years later on that mountainous hike in Northern Thailand that I started to realize the difference between strength and pride—and how, all too often, I think I'm guided by the former when, truthfully, I'm being consumed by the latter.

Whenever I've framed my options as a choice between *either* strength *or* weakness, I'm not leaving myself with much of a choice at all. And so I often prefer to choose the former and live with numbed emotion. I'd rather convince myself that working sixteen-hour days without weekends off or that keeping a stiff upper lip when somebody hurts me is what makes me strong. Seldom do I realize that appearances of strength are actually drawn from a place of pride.

Seeking Justice without Limits

My thrill-seeking, limits-pushing, must-take-the-hardest-route mentality spilled out of my tree-planting framework and into relationships and other facets of my personal life. I've told myself that in anything the hardest route and the greatest amount of effort is always the superior path: *Must work harder at my relationships. Must push faster at personal growth. Must have a stronger and more-inspiring faith.*

This mental boot camp started becoming dangerous when it began seeping into my work in social justice advocacy. Exhibiting all the symptoms of a dehumanized humanitarian, I subconsciously numbed myself from the traumas of life on the field in an attempt to meet the criteria of the quintessentially perseverant justice worker. I wasn't aware my pursuit of limitless strength was draining me until tragedy struck—and it all started with a mosquito.

In a rural Cambodian village one afternoon, one tiny, insignificant, unnoticeable mosquito carrying the *chikungunya* virus (similar to dengue) infected one of my youngest staff members. Sopheap*, a twenty-six-year-old Khmer trainer, had fallen ill and admitted himself to a small, local hospital to treat his symptoms.

I visited him the next day, startled to see him sitting on a dirty hospital mattress in a one-room, open-air building with children from the street running around barefoot between beds. Off in one corner, an elderly woman in a colourful sarong sat on her hands and knees while ironing a stack of her clothes. The most bizarre part was the total absence of doctors or hospital staff demonstrating any kind of medical knowledge. Someone had hooked up Sopheap to an IV without so much as an assessment, hoping that pumping him with fluids would improve his condition.

It didn't.

As I was crawling into bed late a few nights later, one of my English-speaking Khmer staff called me. Over the phone in broken English, she frantically explained that Sopheap had been rushed to the emergency hospital in a city over two hours away. Not knowing whether or not he had a support network there, I quickly assembled a team and drove the treacherous, unlit road to the hospital to visit him.

A few hours later, we'd arrived and headed urgently to the ICU, which was divided from the rest of the hospital by a rusted tin door. With greying skin hanging lifelessly on his fail bones,

---

* Note: Name has been changed.

Sopheap lay motionless in a dilapidated bed, with mangled bodies to his right and left showing little signs of professional care. I quickly realized that, here, the ICU was not where people came to receive the intensive care they needed to get better. Here, the ICU was where people came to die.

With every minute, I could visibly see Sopheap wither away—the first time I'd seen death in such close proximity. An oxygen mask concealed his face, although he was not responding to us anyhow. The only movement he made all night was when he started choking for a brief moment and vomited green liquid. I shocked myself when I realized I was silently praying that God would take him to heaven now without prolonging his pain any further.

Anger rose up in my chest as I watched a couple of doctors standing lazily off in a corner, not seeming terribly concerned that there was a roomful of dying people that could survive with the proper care. But in Cambodia, a virtually lawless society, it wasn't uncommon for doctors to bribe their way to obtaining a medical degree if they could afford it. And innocent people paid the price of their bribery.

The unethical act of doctors donning a lab coat and stethoscope without ever receiving formal training started infuriating me as much as the injustice of watching a twenty-six-year-old man painfully losing his life to a virus that most of the world has never heard the name of before. He was too young and had too much potential for this to happen to him. And I felt helpless.

Drained and a little lost, I called my staff members together after we'd spent some final minutes with Sopheap in a group prayer. Tiredly, I arranged for our team to check into a nearby hotel—the only one in town still open at two in the morning. I lay wide awake in the heat of the night for hours, listening to the squeal of geckos on the walls of the hotel room while focusing my bloodshot eyes on the cellphone on the nightstand. All night, I waited for the hospital to call us to announce Sopheap's death.

Yet the call never came. Early the next morning, my staff members and I rushed to the hospital, finding Sopheap still hooked up to a tangle of wires but propped up a little higher in bed. Below the foggy oxygen mask breathing life into him, he wore the faint smile of a true survivor on his sunken face. His sister and girlfriend, still in the same clothes as the night before, stood teary eyed at his bed.

Sopheap was going to live. He still had a long and arduous recovery before him, with the expectation for residual joint and kidney damage—but the fact that he'd lasted the night was a miracle.

My staff and I drove home with an air of hope. All of us were bleary eyed and exhausted, so when we pulled up to the office a few tiring hours later, I vehemently insisted they all return to their families and take the day off. None of them protested.

I too was wholly depleted. On top of the accumulation of other tragedies I'd witnessed during my time in Cambodia, those twenty-four hours were traumatizing enough to render me incoherent and emotionally debilitated. I was pushing my breaking point, but the voice of the people-pleasing perfectionist in me overruled the voice of reason. Taking time off—even after a traumatizing event—is not an option for people who think they're invulnerable.

I staggered home and gave myself only enough time to put on a strong pot of coffee and change out of my clothes that still carried a lingering smell of disinfectants. Within five minutes, I was back at work with a mug of extra-strong coffee and a forced but weary smile. The remaining staff greeted me pleasantly with puzzled expressions, abiding by the non-confrontational culture of "don't ask, don't tell."

I knew they thought I was certifiably insane for coming into the office after such a traumatic incident. And beneath my robotic default setting, I *was* traumatized. All I wanted to do was break down into tears and stay in bed all day with a soothing cup of hot tea. My body was screaming at me to compensate for the emotional exhaustion and lack of sleep. But I was also conditioned to believe that strong people come into work no matter what. Strong people can practice emotional detachment. Strong people know no limits.

Little did I know that, sooner or later, believing I was invincible would destroy me. Because if all I know is self-sacrifice, there will be no self left to sacrifice at all.

Doing Our Best

As humanitarians, we're prone to glorify self-sacrifice. We're the hiker who refuses to listen to the warning signs from her body. We're the tree planter who chooses injury over boundaries. We're the manager who strives to take care of her staff and save all her clients yet never stops to heal the sting of pain or ease the load of injustice.

At the outset of my journey, I treated boundaries as if they were a deterrent to connecting with the people I came to serve. And so, in my grand foray into humanitarian work in Mexico, I refused to hold back when it came to caring for the children I taught. I was willing to do anything for them—whether or not that was wise on my part.

Julia, my six-year-old student with Down's syndrome, was much more than a child I fed, taught new words to, and changed into clean clothes everyday. She became my life. I was so invested in her that I loved her like my daughter—which perhaps was naive, idealistic, and maybe even inappropriate. But I knew I wasn't the only humanitarian out there who went a little too far out on a limb that it started to crack beneath my weight.

There was my boss at a women's centre I used to work at who allowed women who had been abused by their partners to sleep on her couch until they could find a more permanent place to stay. There were my co-workers who allowed the at-risk youth from their caseloads to text and call them on weekends and evenings when they were having a hard time. I had colleagues who secretly slipped cash to clients who couldn't afford to buy new shoes for their children.

It was a sick kind of solidarity, but we needed to know we weren't alone in confusing our roles. Because on the one hand, we are told that professionalism means being detached, even aloof. On the other hand, we are told that we refute our right to have boundaries by being humanitarians. And so we do both: we reject our own emotions because we only have enough energy for the emotions of the people we're helping;

meanwhile, we assure ourselves that justice requires us to ignore our limits.

Our commitment and our intrepid desires to love and to serve may create an illusion of nobility. We put on a brave face every time we meet up with our students, our clients, our friends, as if our hope is boundless. As if we trust things will get better soon. As if we aren't fearful for the lives our clients live. Behind the veneer of tenacity, though, we're creating a human-made epidemic: a disease of burnout.

We numb. We self-medicate. We develop addictions and resort to whatever coping mechanisms will help us to avoid seeming as if we lack strength or commitment. We take the harder route every single time. We isolate ourselves, denying the help and support of other people. We turn further from the very things that would heal us.

But when that breaking point finally comes—when we're watching a co-worker die on a hospital bed or exercising every last effort to find a missing student—we'll finally have to ask ourselves some questions: Is it okay to have a limit to our compassion? To stop when we've reached our threshold of pain tolerance? To lower the bar a little when we've hit our ultimate low?

As champions of justice, we often convince ourselves it's noble to give help but weakness to receive it. If we can even manage to admit it to ourselves that we need help, we try to save ourselves. We try to do it on our own instead of welcoming others in to give to us their piece of our healing.

At some point, though, we're going to be confronted by our finiteness. And when I was finally confronted by mine, I was both disappointed and relieved. I wanted to be there for my student Julia: for every scraped knee and fall from her bicycle, for every moment of hunger, for every thunderstorm when the dirt floor of her shack became too saturated with water to sleep. But I couldn't. There would come a time when I had to learn I could still seek justice without being crushed by it, if I only learned when to help and when to pass the torch to someone else.

When that finally happened for me, I had some lessons to learn—lessons I'm still figuring out. I'm learning to add powerful words like *enough* and *no* to my vocabulary. I'm learning to put a mental embargo on the ego-fuelled thoughts that propel me forward into a performance in vain. I'm learning to differentiate between when I'm fighting for social justice out of a strength coming from a higher power and when I'm acting out of a pride dwelling within myself. I'm learning to find the humility to take a step back.

It's a battle, especially because the work of justice is never finished. There will never be an end to the opportunities to serve, to help, to give. Continually, I'm tempted to work around the clock in defiance of time, knowing I can never fully accomplish what I need to within the confines of a typical nine-to-five workday. And yet I've discovered that pushing myself to sprint my way through this line of work is counterproductive. Instead, I need to readjust my pace and my expectations of a sphere of work that is not as directly and immediately results based as I'd like it to be.

The key is endurance, not speed. It's more about working steadily than being strong. For me, that starts with identifying my needs. Sometimes that means creating boundaries without remorse. It means reaching out to help others without losing myself. It means knowing their pain without being immobilized by it—to feel hurt without hopelessness. To accept that prioritizing self isn't being selfish. To work hard without overworking. To find a time to rest and replenish.

Most of all, it means dwelling in community, not trying to exist in a vacuum. In my darkest times, my closest friends and family carried me through because they could see what I couldn't. Whenever I tried to explain how I'd rather love my clients to pieces than give only a part of myself, my family suggested that no matter how lovingly I may take on other people's burdens, the ensuing exhaustion might undo my efforts. Whenever I tried to defend how uncomfortable I was with the thought of putting a cap on the amount I invested in others, my friends gently reminded me how my ability to endure hinged on being able to say no when it counted. They spoke truth and reality into my life when I needed it most.

Leaning into community meant being able to get the help I needed to exit the vicious cycle of unbounded giving and living. It's where I learned to be vulnerable—which is perhaps the greatest lesson of all. Because it's hard to trust someone who shows no signs of fragility, no traces of imperfection, no indications of fallibility.

Those who suffer don't want a hero; they want a human—a genuine, real person who can join them in the wonder and woes of common humanity. Someone who knows what it's like to be bound by limitations. Someone who also struggles and surrenders, feels, and fails. Someone who knows that maybe it really is about doing the best we can after all.

Letting Go

For most of my life, I thought limits existed to be pushed. Any obstacles in my path were there to be defied, not to deter. And the results were disastrous.

As it turns out, the battlefield is no place for a human to permanently live. Instead, I think a life well lived is one where you know when to fight in the trenches and when to retreat, when to go to war and when to live in peace. It's exhibiting more courage than strength: the courage to be vulnerable, the courage to lean into support and collaboration, the courage to ask for help.

Maybe there are times when we need to put wisdom before martyrdom—like throwing somebody a life vest before diving in to save them. Maybe having limits to the lengths we're willing to go to help someone isn't selfish; maybe it's what sustains our journey. Maybe our limits aren't there to tell us "you can't" but there to tell us "you shouldn't."

Yes, we need people who will be committed to justice for the long haul, who are willing to go the extra mile every now and then, but we need those same people to have the wisdom to know there are times when all we can do is our best. There are times when we can't save everyone. There are times when we have to be okay with being human.

Katie Bergman

It's easy to mistake pride for strength. It's often less painful to hide behind the grandeur of bravery than to reveal our vulnerable, authentic selves. But when our pride looks like strength, we will never accomplish what we need to.

Sometimes, being strong means holding on. Other times, it means letting go.

CHAPTER 10

A New Kind of Honour: Learning to Walk Away

Ruin and recovery are both from within.
—Epictetus

Unbeknownst to me at the time, my term in Cambodia was guiding me toward a radically different way of seeking justice.

Contrary to what many of my acquaintances imagined, it would not come in the form of some heroic endeavour or a grandiose accomplishment. It would not be an epic moment—nothing like Frodo destroying the One Ring or Atticus Finch defending justice in *To Kill a Mockingbird.* It would be neither glamorous nor well received. And it would happen at a moment hardly anybody would call noble—at a moment of my greatest vulnerability: when I walked away.

Perhaps a victorious parting of the clouds or a wave of thunderous applause would've punctuated the rightness of my choice. Or maybe that arduous walk would've been more assuring had the musical score from a Peter Jackson movie played in the background instead of the clamouring drumbeat of my opponent's disapproval. Instead, my decision was completely countercultural to the humanitarian world—not at all a traditional act of martyrdom. It would be unedited and uncomfortable. It would be chaotic, humbling, and lonely. In the messy aftermath of acting on what I perceived to be just, there would be only me—alone, unarmed, and depleted.

It started halfway through my year in Cambodia, when something frightening began happening to me. After months of my energy slowly burning out, fragments of my memory started fading out too.

Every time I got on my motorbike, I could feel the droplets of rain pelted against my body by a relentless wind. I could hear the competing voices of *tuk tuk* drivers yelling drunkenly at each other. I could see the chapped and weathered hands of land-mine survivors reaching out to me in a desperate request for spare change. And yet I couldn't recall exactly how I'd managed to get to my destination, how I'd somehow weaved my way through throngs of noisy vehicles and hand-pulled carts—or my purpose for driving anywhere in the first place.

I was so drained that I would forget why I was standing in the doorway of the finance office at work or why I was holding a staff meeting. Parts of my mind still functioned, but other parts were blank. I could manage to mechanically compile statistics, submit reports on time, plan media campaigns, follow up with staff on their projects, and write proposals—but I couldn't remember if I had eaten or slept, what day it was, or how my dishes had been washed and put away. Reality began colliding with my subconscious, and I started confusing what I had dreamt and what was real. On a few occasions, when my mind and body were too tired to press on, I would physically collapse in a heap of helplessness.

Sleep became an unsafe place. The traumas I'd seen would hijack my subconscious and replay over and over again in my mind like some sort of torturous merry-go-round I couldn't disembark. Nightmares haunted me, leaving me in pools of sweat and sudden panic attacks in the middle of the night.

Had I been a little less exhausted and a little more alert, I would've been frightened that I was suffering from early-onset Alzheimer's or some tropical illness. But I was far past the point of being able to feel concerned. I spent all my energy worrying about my staff, my clients, my deadlines—there just wasn't any worry left over for me.

Every night as I returned to a dark and empty house, I passed by a refrigerator magnet that I'd been given at my two-week orientation session at the start of the year. On the magnet was a catchy slogan about how much my organization promoted self-care. It was a symbol of the supportive safety net my organization had promised me months and months ago but seemed to have forgotten about. And if there was any room left for bitterness, I would've felt it. I would've wondered how I'd allowed myself to be so duped into thinking I was going to be supported in this line of work by my company. I would've wondered if member care was nothing more than a fridge magnet.

Piece by piece, I gradually started to realize I was in no position to single-handedly support a fragile community of people. How could I help others when I could barely help myself?

Running on Empty

You can sell your soul to anything. You can sell it to the interminable climb up the corporate ladder as easily as selling it trying to become somebody's hero within a humanitarian organization. In my case, I gave away my childhood whimsy and zest for an awestruck life to the cause of justice in a way that God never intended.

After years of construing a sick sort of nobility out of missional self-sacrifice, I wound up trapped and terrified in Cambodia, asking myself, *Does my worth come from trying to become a hero—or is my worth inherent as a human, created carefully and uniquely for the purpose to love and be loved?*

My own confusion of strength and pride often meant I was more likely to push myself to the breaking point in my service than ask for help when I needed it most. Shielding myself with a facade of ironclad strength meant I could act as if the weight of my work didn't interfere with my happiness or disrupt my peace of mind. I could pretend to be a fearless martyr, exempted from the emotional heaviness of justice advocacy and the exhaustion of nomadic living.

It became more challenging to appear invincible, however, when I started realizing it wasn't only our client base experiencing trauma and abuse. Increasingly, I became aware of how the injustices these projects fought against were tearing apart the lives of my own staff as well.

While I had grown up with my own set of struggles—mainly involving the melodrama of teenage vindictiveness in junior high—my staff had grown up in a genocide. Some of them could still remember the sounds of land mines exploding in the distance or the shrill cry of their mothers shouting for them to come back inside their hut before the Khmer Rouge army would find them first.

The closer I grew to my staff during my year in Cambodia, the more some of them started sharing intimate details of their personal lives: of being orphaned, beaten, and forced to work as child labourers. Some of my male staff had illegally crossed the border into Thailand to beg for food or to work for pennies, only to be trafficked into demeaning and dangerous work on a fishing boat or a construction site without pay. Some of my female staff had been excommunicated because they broke off an engagement—or they bitterly chose to suffer in a loveless arranged marriage within the cultural confines that limited and even prohibited female agency.

I knew I was way above my head when one of my youngest staff members in her late twenties came into my office in tears, telling me her husband was drinking again and had disappeared with all their savings after an explosive fight. She didn't have enough money to buy milk for her baby girl, let alone to afford the rent for her dilapidating apartment. I was the only person she could come to for support.

I felt helpless. At twenty-three, I was still growing into adulthood. I hardly possessed the wisdom to know what *I* would do in these situations, let alone the ability to provide support and counselling to others. Every night, I would return home from work feeling more empty than fulfilled, more discouraged than hopeful—too crushed from all the bad to feel encouraged by any of the good.

While studying justice as an undergrad, I learned how helping can go terribly awry. I learned about the invasive voluntourism programs for Westerners to visit orphanages in Southeast Asia and how the Structural Adjustment Programs implemented by the IMF and World Bank ended up crippling economies of developing nations even more than helping them. Outside academia, I knew how much popular media thrives on sinking its teeth into juicy stories of failed humanitarian efforts. Even my own organization in Cambodia loved to preach the principles of "do no harm," citing cases of the unintended damage caused by other non-governmental organizations while bypassing acknowledgement of their own faulty outreaches and failed strategies.

I heard plenty about when helping hurts communities. What I heard less about was how helping can hurt the helper. Somehow it's easier to point out flaws and criticize another entity than to admit how much of a toll this line of work takes on those at the front lines.

So at twenty-three I decided that perhaps now was the time to start talking about it.

After a great deal of coaching and coaxing from trusted mentors and family members, I came to the humbling conclusion that I couldn't go on any longer like this. It would kill me to leave this work behind, but it was also killing me to stay.

Once I accepted that something needed to change, I approached my boss—not as an appeal for sympathy but as an opportunity to restructure how our organization treated its staff. In an emotional meeting with him, I explained the trickle-down effect of how a demoralized team of program managers spread thinly across too many projects would eventually affect the projects themselves. As a burning-out manager, I told him I couldn't exercise the patience to nurture, support, and motivate my staff to carry out high-quality, crucial services that were protecting children, families, and schools from violence and exploitation. Something needed to change, I told him.

I didn't broach the conversation with high expectations from my boss. I figured the best-case scenario would be that he'd demonstrate consistency in upholding the values I'd heard glorified at orientation about promoting staff care. At minimum, I'd hoped he'd offer some helpful advice, institute practical training, or even grant me the vacation time he was supposed to have approved over a month ago.

He gave me no such response. Instead, his words lacerated my last shred of hope for help: "Well, Katie, it really is a harsh world out there. You're just going to have to try harder."

And finally, I did what I should have months earlier: I said no.

Walking Away

Letting go was complicated. As an uncompromising perfectionist, I struggled to reconcile the fact that I was quitting—the first time I'd ever quit something in my life.

In my work, I constantly heard messages about Jesus calling his followers to pick up their crosses and follow him, regardless of the cost. I interpreted this to mean that my job was to seek out the heaviest, thorniest, most cumbersome cross.

Splinters and pain weren't by-products according to this biblical interpretation—they were the objective.

And so I always pushed myself to work harder, longer, faster—because, as a humanitarian, as a person of faith, that's where I believed worth to come from. To serve is to suffer. To be a humanitarian is to experience extreme levels of adversity. Hard work is earmarked by tribulations. Justice advocacy is incompatible with such trite affairs as happiness and recreation.

For me, the problem was that the more I tried to lug around the most burdensome cross I could find, the more exhausted and cynical I became. Forging my way down the hardest route wasn't building my character as I expected but eroding it. It was leaving me with *less* of a capacity to serve, love, and grow.

It took a painful experience of burnout for me to see that something's terribly wrong when my badge of honour is hitting that sixteenth hour of work. When suffering for the cause is the hallmark of being a humanitarian. When busyness is glorified and rest is condemned. When justice can only be pursued with a bleeding heart, a burdened mind, and a martyr's demeanour.

I'd always heard that God wanted me to suffer. Seldom had I heard that God also wanted me to thrive, to enjoy the simple pleasures and beauty that God had created for us to appreciate, to be whole.

It was time for me to let go of the shock from spending my life pursuing something that left me jaded and crushed. I had to let go of all the words of praise people had said to me and let go of how their words had reinforced my decision to ardently persevere. I needed to let go because the same opportunity that had promised to harmonize my passion with the practice of it had become dramatically incongruent with my moral-driven convictions.

No longer could I try to find belonging within an organization that upheld the celebrity status of the organization before the survival status of those it served. No longer could I participate in a for-profit endeavour under a non-profit guise. I'd become too tired—not tired *of* seeking justice but tired *from* seeking justice at a pace I could never sustain. Too tired from trying to prevail in an environment where my personal needs and values were considered insignificant—and even selfish—when weighed against the overarching cause.

Once my environment had became so shrouded with poisoned motives and corrupted actions, I saw that leaving was not about selfishness or stubbornly having principles for the sake of principles. It was realizing I no longer wanted to parade around with a sceptre of justice to my own detriment, not to mention the detriment of others. It was moving toward a place of reclaiming my health and happiness.

It was a matter of honour.

A New Kind of Honour

For some, honour is perseverance at any cost. Doing what is "honourable" is ranked on the same scale as nobility, with the anticipation of immediate gratification for intrepid behaviour. It's glorified martyrdom.

We usually don't get rewarded for being honourable to *ourselves*. We don't receive gilded trophies for acting upon our personal values or for doing what we believe to be right and true when it challenges the status quo. But this was exactly what my experience of honour looked like. It didn't feature the strengths I'd worked so hard to hone but emphasized the fallibilities I'd tried so hard to hide. Instead of honour emerging from soldiering on with tenacity, I found it in the vulnerable act of walking away.

Making a coming-of-age decision driven by my own brand of honour wouldn't end up looking quite the same as it did in a Hollywood film or a fantasy novel. That's because we live in an age of berating the act of quitting. We believe regrets are the worst thing that could happen to us. We look down upon people who are honest about what they can and can't tolerate.

But in my case, regretting the length of my stay in Cambodia was one of the best things that has ever happened to me. It meant being able to finally remove the false veneer of invincibility—which was the most meaningful way I could live honourably. For the first time, engaging in an honourable act wasn't putting on a suit of armour and wielding a sword. It wasn't trying to cover up the dehumanized humanitarian in me with a facade of martyrdom. It was pure disarmament.

I *did* give up—I just didn't give in.

As it turns out, it's not that I needed to leave the justice sphere completely. I just needed redirection. I needed a different kind of devotion, a kind of devotion that would accommodate a vast scope of factors—like my health and well-being. I needed to walk away from masochistic motivations and toward a more peaceful purpose.

In the wake of one of my most surrendering life experiences, living with a new understanding of honour has since been a journey closer in the direction of freedom, authenticity, and wholeness. It has meant recalibrating the visions and dreams I tucked away from childhood, awakening the essence of my human design. It has meant re-imagining what could be, not simply pursuing what already is. It has meant no longer having to be a hero who saves but to simply be a human who helps.

Honour, as I'm learning, is something you have but must work to keep. It is something that cannot be taken away from you unless you allow it. And it is something that is born not only out of noble ambition or self-sacrifice but of stripped-down, straight-up authenticity.

Especially in the face of opposition, honour is the courage to be who we really are—even if that means walking away from who we believed we were supposed to be.

CHAPTER 11

Care for the Caregiver: Secure Your Mask before Assisting Others

Keep peace within yourself, then you
can also bring peace to others.
—Kempis

The sky was a heavy curtain of grey, enveloping the entire runway of the Siem Reap International Airport in a cold and smothering embrace.

Something about the sky felt artificial. All I'd known of the Cambodian sky was a blue, sunny, cloudless celestial sphere, except for the brief intermission during monsoon season when it rained relentlessly for an hour or two every afternoon. Today's haze of dark clouds and fog felt disconcertingly appropriate. It was my perfect metaphor. The sky was burnout personified: ominous and blank while stifling even a single stream of light from passing through its steely barrier—and I was the inconsequential plane, trapped beneath the heavy coating of gloomy clouds.

Climbing the steps onto the Angkor Air plane with what little energy I had left, I refused to allow myself to fix my eyes one last time on the rice fields and palm trees I had seen every day for nearly a year in Cambodia. The beauty of the landscape brought me no comfort when this was the place that had broken me to irreparable pieces. This was a desperate attempt to escape from my Alcatraz. There was no looking back.

As I settled into my seat, preparing for the first leg of a long journey, I half-listened as the flight attendant rattled off the safety procedures for our flight: *"In case there is a loss in cabin pressure, yellow oxygen masks will deploy from the ceiling compartment located above you."*

For so long, I'd been in need of an oxygen mask of my own. Even a year ago when I'd flown into this same airport in Siem Reap for the first time, I had already been dangerously low on air. Weary from years of focusing on trying to be an agent of help and healing. Derailed by forgetting my own need for those same things.

Without leaving any room for concern of my own needs or safety, I'd set myself up for failure. Instead of balancing helping with health and responsibility with rest, I'd gone full tilt on an extreme of giving what little I had left to my humanitarian service. And it had ended with me escaping from Cambodia like a fugitive, with one final shred of hope for my own self-initiated rescue.

"To secure, pull the mask toward you, secure the elastic strap to your head, and fasten it so it covers your mouth and nose. Breathe normally."

It had been months since I'd been able to breathe normally. My chest was now an empty cage, devoid of a heartbeat and unable to process normal, cleansing breathing patterns. Especially when I jolted awake after another nightmare, my chest would be so tight it felt as though all the air had been permanently squeezed out of me.

Somewhere between my list of connections in Ho Chi Minh and Tokyo and Chicago, I hoped my breath would return to me. I prayed my heart would start beating again by the time I flew into my final destination, before my family waiting at the Winnipeg airport would see me in this despairing condition. My parents in particular had been through enough torment by hearing about how poorly I was doing through partly censored emails and Skype calls—I didn't want them to have to see it too.

"Even if the bag does not inflate, please keep in mind that oxygen is still flowing."

Hope, as I'd learned that year, was a hard pill to swallow while living in darkness. In a country like Cambodia, where there were few signs of redemption on the horizon, hope seemed too stale, too vapid to be a productive use of my energy and emotion. Whether it was trying to support my soft-spoken Khmer friend who couldn't leave her abusive husband in a culture that rebuked divorce or seeing hundreds of malnourished women filing out of garment factories with bandanas wrapped around their faces, earning slightly over one dollar for a full day's work—hope seemed feeble at best and dangerous at worst.

Based on any of the tangible indicators of sight and sound and touch, I boarded that plane without a fragment of optimism. How could there be any validity in hoping when I couldn't breathe, couldn't feel, couldn't even think clearly? As desperately as I wanted to trust that restoration was at work, I figured I was too far gone for things to get better.

"Please make sure to secure your own mask before assisting others."

My head snapped up from its blank gaze at my feet, fully attentive for the first time for the flight attendant's toneless monologue. In my life as a traveller, I had walked through dozens of airports, boarded hundreds of flights, and heard the same safety speech in countless accents and languages—but today, I was hearing this speech for the first time.

As the flight attendant finished the safety speech in English and began reciting it in Khmer, something within me began to dispel the guilt I'd carried with me onto the plane as I prepared to leave Cambodia behind. The glorified martyrdom complex I'd always operated under as a humanitarian suddenly lost its appeal to me. In fact, it seemed not only counterproductive but also foolish. How could I expect to bring life-giving help to somebody if I myself was struggling to breathe?

I thought about the pilot for a moment, finishing the pre-takeoff checklist and preparing to push back the plane at any moment. If for any reason the pilot's abilities had been compromised to safely fly that plane, would I have still pressured him or her to fly? Would I really prefer that a pilot, with hundreds of human lives in his or her care, choose to fly 450 tons of aluminum at 35,000 feet in a state of exhaustion? Or would I rather the pilot humbly relinquish his or her duties and be replaced by somebody who had the stamina to do the job safely and well?

Nobody wants a tired pilot. Why would a tired humanitarian be any different?

While the plane backed away from the airport and further into the cloudy abyss, I wondered to myself how the last few years of my life might have been different if I had practiced securing my own mask before assisting others.

Filling Our Own Wells

Years earlier, at the end of every summer of tree planting, I would return home to modern civilization with a conspicuous farmer's tan and scrapes from my toes to my eyebrows, ready to be bombarded with the same bewildered question from people: "How do you make yourself plant trees all day long?"

I knew the most well-received answer would be to claim I was driven by a tenacious desire to save the environment. But that would be false. Because to be honest, there's got to be more than a zeal for Greenpeace activism motivating me to plant flimsy pine seedlings while hanging from the cliff of a mountain with a swarm of black flies and mosquitoes trying to attack me before a grizzly bear does. As much as I wish I could say being part of a cause was enough incentive, the truth is it never was.

Another popular response would be to assure people that I stayed motivated because of the reward waiting for me at the end of the day: the thrill of creating a new personal record, the smug satisfaction of finding out I'd out-planted some of the boys, but most of all the number of digits on my pay stub. But that would also be untrue. With workers being paid per tree, planting may seem to be a magical ratio of hard work being equally proportionate to income earned. But that wasn't the case on days when our truck sank into a four-foot-deep mud hole and we were stranded along an unmarked road, wasting hours we could otherwise have been making money. Or when we spent full mornings hiking up cratered logging roads and trudging through knee-deep mud to get to a worksite that a 4x4 truck can't drive through, leaving only a fraction of time to plant barely enough trees to cover the daily camp costs deducted from each paycheque.

It was more than money. It was more than the glory of saving the planet. In the three summers I spent living in the bush, earning a dime for every weighted squat to plant a tree, I can tell you exactly what helps a tree planter to push through the day: food.

Peanut-butter sandwiches, swallowed in two giant bites and downed with a litre of Gatorade, are what fuels this unique species of human to plant upwards of two, three, or even four thousand trees in a single day. A square of puffed wheat cake and a bag of double-chocolate-chip cookies waiting in a tree planter's lunch box are the incentives that drive him or her to pulverize through tumultuous land that mandates a complicated ratio of pine and spruce trees interspersed 2.99 metres apart through ominous fields of devil's club, stinging nettle, and poison ivy.

As a foreman during my final summer of tree planting, I strategically utilized the stimulus of food to propagate greater efficiency and productivity in my planters. I would stock up on chocolate bars during our trips to the city over the weekends and sneak them under the Silvicool tarps that shaded my planters' trees and lunches during the daytime. Once, I watched from a distance as one of my burliest tree planters gleefully unwrapped his chocolate bar like a Christmas present, swallowed it whole, and then went out and pounded five hundred trees into the ground in less than forty minutes.

Food—without a doubt—has always been a prime incentive for planters to work hard over a one-day shift. But food on its own doesn't compensate for the disasters that happen—like when a tree planter accidentally drives her shovel into a hornet's nest that explodes into an army of merciless stinging beasts, sending her back to the first-aid tent with swollen limbs and a bruised ego. It doesn't quell the heart of a rookie tree planter who is madly searching for a way to stage an accident to break his arm so that he has a sufficient excuse to quit without compromising his pride or reputation.

For me, food was a good motivator in the short-term, but it never offered enough comfort to balance out the rough-and-tumble lifestyle of a nomadic tree planter. It didn't make up for missing summertime weddings or not being able to attend my own convocation ceremony because our camp was too far away from the nearest airport. It didn't provide the long-term motivation I needed to keep going day after day, through sheets of rain or pelts of hail or relentless heat that dried up everyone's water supply by noon.

After a year or two of tree planting, I realized it wasn't the cause itself or the immediate rewards or the temporary pleasures that kept me going. It was the litany of simple but significant joys: the intangible beauty of community, the majesty of untamed nature, the unlimited opportunities for growth and self-reflection.

It was the campfire at the end of the day that warmed chapped hands and spurred storytelling and laughter to the soundtrack of an acoustic guitar or bongo drums. It was the cleansing shower after work that was worth all three minutes of hot water that the generator could produce. It was the side-splitting laughter from impromptu cartwheel competitions, roadside dance parties, and stacking up as many people as physics allows in a piggyback race. It was the lazy days off spent sprawled in a grassy park or resting sore muscles in a hot tub at a small-town pool.

What pushes us through? It's the multiple sources of bliss that give impetus for the back-breaking journey of one who plants trees that will one day become forests.

The Things That Help Us on Our Way

As I gradually outgrew tree planting and began pursuing a vocation in community development and justice advocacy, people continued to ask a similar question: "How do you push yourself all day long to fight for justice?"

Early on, my response would always contain the assurance that being part of a "good cause" was enough. Knowing I was working tirelessly to be an agent of change in a broken world was what propelled me forward into years of living among the most-desperate and most-deprived people I'd ever encountered. Yet the more I strived with the Cause as my catalyst and my singular source of purpose, the more quickly I lost myself.

Introduced to a theology of unrestricted sacrificial giving, I learned from the Cause that my work required my full allegiance.

This, of course, meant that anything distracting even a fraction of my attention from full-time service was a selfish endeavour.

I learned by reinforcement that taking even fifteen-minute lunch breaks wasn't worth the scornful stares and guilt-inducing comments from veteran co-workers. The hoops I had to jump through in order to take well-earned vacation time wasn't worth the punishment from militant supervisors who thought that going three years without any time off was something to boast about.

As I dug deeper into my work in the non-profit realm, I met a lot of humanitarians like me who had good intentions and solid work ethics but met few who still had spirit. Everywhere I looked, I saw burnout. In the painstaking journey of being integrated into the expectations of the Cause, too many service workers had lost their joy and passion along the way. Like me, they had also lost their sense of self in pursuit of a greater purpose. I suspected much of this loss of zest was because they too had been told their work was about others, not about them—that any positive personal return or tangential reward was simply a bonus.

By drawing everything it can from fervent humanitarians, the Cause gets exactly what it asks for: impressive statistics on the number of wells built, emergency food packs distributed, and restoration homes built; sizable donations raised from campaigns that demanded weeks of skipped meals and sleepless nights from the fundraising team working at minimum wage; heartwarming success stories reported by resolute social workers living in developing countries to be used as promotional material plastered across the home page of the website and featured on the front page of the annual report.

Demanding martyrdom from its ferociously loyal intermediaries may be the easiest way for the Cause to reach goals and hit targets in the short term, but it also creates a barrage of ulcers, anxiety, and breakdowns in the long term. It severs relationships wherever the Cause is expected to be more of a priority than one's partner, spouse, or family. It develops into unhealthy coping mechanisms that lead to poor habits, which lead to addictions, which lead to depression … Are the long-term repercussions of the short-term successes really worth it?

For myself, I want to believe the products of my labour have been worthwhile, but my labour came at too high of a price. When my choice to serve others meant having nothing left over to invest in my own heart, health, and happiness, it seemed I was committing a disservice. My attempt to bring light to someone else's life through martyrdom led to my own life becoming dark and ugly and hopeless.

Eventually, I needed to turn to my roster of personal advisors to help convince me that something needed to change. One mentor put my struggle with glorifying martyrdom into perspective with one short sentence: "Katie, what's happening here is that we're killing the goose that lays the golden eggs."

Once I realized my mentor wasn't calling me a web-footed fowl, the meaning behind his metaphor sunk deep into my heart. It was the first time I sincerely believed somebody who told me that my human value exceeded my work productivity—and that maybe my value was worth protecting.

We Get the Love We Think We Deserve

By the end of my time Cambodia, I was too bitter to do anything else but blame my organization for reducing me to a state of fragility and emptiness. It was far easier to accuse some other entity for my misery than to examine some problematic source within myself. But the truth is, I probably wouldn't have allowed anybody else to beat me into the ground unless I felt deserving of it.

A year after I left Cambodia and started working with youth in the inner city of Winnipeg, I began seeing in them what I needed to see in myself. I could visibly see the damage in the eyes of a fifteen-year-old girl who had accepted a lifetime of mistreatment because nobody had ever presented her with an alternative. Many of these youth searched for love and belonging by joining gangs, tolerating the associated violence as a part of the initiation process. Several of the teenage girls I worked with sought it in men a decade or two older than them, not realizing these men were in lust, not in love. Even the youth who were abused or exploited by members of their families kept returning home after running away or spending time in juvie, because that was the only place they received attention—even if that attention was channelled through violence.

With low self-esteem and no other frame of reference, most of them believed this was what they deserved. This was as good as it got. This was love.

Every youth in crisis who sat in the blue plastic chair in my office drew out a sort of unexpected empathy. When I'd applied for this job, I had been concerned I would have little to offer these youth who were mostly Aboriginal and came from homes with neglect, addiction, and abuse, where there wasn't enough money to provide three square meals a day. As a white, educated woman from a middle-class family, who was I to try to be a mentor to them?

Eventually, I had to let go of my divisive approach. After all, I could never empathize when I was dichotomizing "them" as low-income youth and "me" as a privileged white woman. When I related to the youth in my office on a purely human level, I discovered we had more in common than I thought. I had never experienced the kind of abuse they had, so I knew I could never fully identify with them. And yet I too knew what it was like to think I wasn't worthy of the best.

While growing up, I heard in Sunday school many times that Jesus wants us to "love our neighbour as ourselves." The problem was that those Sunday school classes never came with lessons on how to love myself too. And so, many times in my life, I said no to happiness because I didn't think I'd earned it and said yes to maltreatment. I actively sought out pain to be a better service provider because I thought it would allow me to resonate more with the people I worked with. I sought out pain because I didn't think I deserved any better. Seeing myself as a substandard human meant I expected substandard treatment from other people.

When my mentor back in Cambodia broke through to me by suggesting that burdening humanitarians with the expectation of perfection and heroism was like "killing the goose that lays the golden eggs," I finally started engaging with my justice work from a place of worthiness. Not only did my efforts have value, but I also started seeing that, as a person, I have value too.

Not only did my clients deserve compassion, but I deserved compassion too. Not only did the youth I worked with need to love themselves, but I needed to learn to love myself too.

For most of my life, I always regarded compassion as a uni-dimensional expression of empathy and altruism for another person. According to my superiors, humanitarian service is an innately one-sided relationship of give and take. Most of our donors and supporters regard compassion as a commodity of unlimited supply. And so those of us in the trenches of justice work are expected to be Pez dispensers of mercy and justice, mechanically giving out charitable acts like candy. Eventually, humanitarianism no longer comes from a place of compassion but of expectation. It turns service into a job and benevolence into obligation.

We may enter into this work for selfless motives, but that doesn't mean we can give all of ourselves without moments of replenishing. In fact, I'm starting to believe that the caregiving nature of humanitarian work requires even more self-care for those who serve. We need to permit justice workers to embrace their humanity before heroism. We need caregivers who can serve lovingly, deeply, and emphatically, instead of breeding a generation of dehumanized humanitarians.

Perhaps we can't always expect that level of support from our bosses or co-workers. Perhaps it's even unrealistic to demand our partners, families, and friends to fully give us the care we need. Perhaps that replenishing comes from a spiritual place within us that no external source can provide. Perhaps it comes down to us.

Securing My Own Oxygen Mask First

My plane taxied down the tarmac at the Siem Reap airport and moved next into position for takeoff. Resting my heavy head against the window, I gazed out at the thick, clouded skies that kept us enclosed in a dome of grey and repeated the line in my head once more: *"Secure your own mask before assisting others."*

The engines roared, and the plane lurched forward at 140 miles an hour, pushing me back into my chair with gentle force. I watched the gap widening between the ground and our plane as we gained altitude and pointed toward the solid expanse of thick grey clouds.

For a moment, my mind was more preoccupied with the flight attendant's safety speech than with the excitement that I was finally heading home. I was too busy wishing she'd been there at the beginnings of my justice training, warning me that there will be times when I need to secure my mask before trying to assist others. I wish she'd been there when I'd first started buying into the belief that my needs didn't matter. I wish she'd been there when my boss had told me it was my Christian duty to stay longer than my original commitment to become a project manager of twenty staff at age twenty-three. I wish she'd been there when I'd developed an ulcer from working sixteen-hour days without rest because I thought my work was more important than my well-being.

At this point, I couldn't undo the harm I'd done to myself in thinking I wasn't worthy of self-compassion. But I was listening now. I was hearing that it's not possible to try to fill somebody else's well when my own well has run dry. It's not wise for people who have burned out and lost their passion to keep forcing themselves to give from what they do not have. Self-compassion is what creates a reservoir for compassion for others.

Maybe seeking justice doesn't have to be independent of the feeling of joy and the experience of laughter. Maybe living well doesn't need to be diametrically opposed to living meaningfully. Maybe work that's solely based on the expectations or needs of others has lost its meaning—and maybe there's room for my needs, values, and dreams in my work after all.

As a new mantra began placating my mind, the plane disappeared into the engulfment of clouds for only a moment and then broke into a vivid blue sky with a sun burning so brightly I had to shield my eyes. Hidden by the veil of grey had been a beautiful day waiting to be discovered as we ascended, dispelling the illusion of darkness with streams of light guiding me home.

CHAPTER 12

Why I Stayed:
How the Good Exceeds the Bad

The wound is the place where light enters you.
—Rumi

When the plane touched down on Canadian soil—two full days after making my exodus from Cambodia—I half-expected to feel lighter, as if I'd left my burdens somewhere in the stratosphere above the Pacific Ocean. After all, I knew I was safe now. I knew my family was waiting for me at the international arrivals gate inside the Winnipeg airport. But despite the change of scenery and team of support, there was still a long road of recovery ahead of me.

My first few months of being back in Canada were surprisingly painful—not only for me but also for whoever had to watch me. I hardly remember anything of those first three weeks. Everything blurred together in my foggy recollection, except for the vague memory of spending my days staring out the window at the gentle waves lapping against the rocky shore at my parents' lakeside home while curled up in a rocking chair. As friends gradually found out I was safely back home in Canada, my parents were kept busy screening their phone calls and assuring them I'd have the energy to call back in a few weeks.

But even after months of focused recovery, I still had no energy, no appetite, no dexterity, nearly no memory of what had happened the day before. I nearly jumped out of my own skin when anybody made a sudden movement. Sleep was more exhausting than refreshing since nightmares held my subconscious captive and tormented me throughout the night. My nerves were too shot to tolerate any noise, even music softly playing in the background—something that had been fundamental to my former life.

The worst part of it all was that I couldn't access any of the remedies I knew I needed to get better. The coping mechanisms I used to rely upon—writing, running, diving into a creative project, reading an inspiring book—all required a vigour I didn't have. Above all, I needed to surround myself with positive people and talk through my pain with them, but I'd lost the vitality required to carry a basic conversation or string together a coherent sentence. I couldn't be around more than one or two people at one time without cringing. All I could do was sit and gently pendulate back and forth in the rocking chair, wondering if I would ever forget.

Seeing me in such poor shape, the people closest to me began calling my vocation into question. Some lovingly expressed their concern for me and gently tried to steer me to easier, safer, less-exhausting work closer to home. Some begged I take a lengthy break. Some even boldly suggested I permanently leave justice behind.

To them, I looked like somebody enmeshed in an abusive relationship. It was a one-sided, isolating affiliation with a controlling and possessive partner who demanded my exclusive attention, sequestering me from other people. My family and friends had seen the dominating behaviours and power tactics used by this grand manipulator who knew how to wield guilt and threats to keep me in line, to keep me loyal. They saw me as someone living in a servile state, knowing there would be criticism and punishment if I chose to assert my own will or needs.

Yes, I had been beaten down and disillusioned by my calling. Yes, I often felt as though I was trying to justify an abusive and maniacal relationship by rationalizing the pain and protecting the abuser. I could understand their confusion. After all, how could a "true calling" generate so much agony for somebody without an appetite for fame and fortune but for peace and justice?

Maybe there was some element of ego and taking pride in martyrdom and feeling shame for having boundaries that kept me fighting for justice. But there was more to it than that. So how could I explain that the dream I'd had by the time I was seven years old had led me to such heartbreak? Most of all, how could I justify how drawn I felt to continue honouring that dream?

The Value of the Good

As a humanitarian, the majority of my days are not filled with feel-good victories and success stories. On the contrary, if I were to divide seeking justice into categories of either good or bad outcomes, then my own experience of seeking justice would look fairly grim. I'd have to assign it a good-to-bad ratio of about ten to ninety: About 10 percent of what I do feels good, seems edifying, and looks productive. The remaining 90 percent is comprised of about 40 percent stress and chaos, 30 percent mundanity, 15 percent bitterness and disillusionment, and 5 percent downright atrociousness.

And to be honest, even that 10 percent of feel-good outcomes aren't Nobel Peace Prize moments. They're not rescuing dozens of underage girls from brothels in Bangkok or bringing a community of Syrian refugees to safety. Sometimes it's the most simple, ordinary, and unheralded moments that keep me doing what I do.

It's watching the dirt-encrusted faces of migrant children in Mexico light up in delight because I let them use my camera to take pictures of the wild turkeys roaming in the middle of their barbed-wire camp. It's being moved to tears by the radiant glow of beaming former prostitutes on their graduation day to celebrate two years of sobriety, dressed not as hookers but as princesses. It's catching a co-worker carefully dishing out the best vegetables in a soup for a prostituted woman—and although my mind is tired, my body is shivering, and my heart is heavy from walking the streets of the red light district, my heart swells from the tender act of gentle compassion.

It's those unexpected moments of humour and connection. It's being halfway through an attempt to discipline a misbehaving nine-year-old student with ADHD when his stoic face breaks into a grin and he abruptly bursts into a montage of dance moves and I can't help but laugh and pause to appreciate his unbreakable spirit and irreverent sense of humour. It's when I'm struggling to articulate myself in a foreign language in the middle of an intense meeting about domestic violence and rape and my frustration with trying to communicate with my co-worker pushes me to the brink of hilarity—and then both of us are laughing hysterically to tears, in the one language we both speak fluently.

However infrequent, however unremarkable, it's those moments of raw humanity and unadulterated beauty that somehow make it all worthwhile.

Listening for the Beautiful

There is an obvious value in the moments when seeking justice prevails—when that one chronically unemployed homeless client finally finds a job and can keep an apartment. Or when a sixteen-year-old high-school dropout makes the decision to remove his gang tattoos and to finish school. But first of all, let it be known that those moments are neither normal nor immediate outcomes. And secondly, as hard as it can be to accept sometimes, even within chaotic moments of frustration, stress, and discouragement comes a different kind of value too.

When a life is dedicated to seeing the most-bleak and most-horrifying experiences of injustice, you can't help but be quick to notice when the pure, beautiful, and touching acts of humanity come. For me, I think it's *because* of the ugliness that I cherish moments of tenderness and unforeseen grace even more.

I've seen how bad life can get—and so, ironically, I live with an even greater appreciation for how precious life is too. In fact, one of the most unexpectedly beautiful days I've ever had was the day my wallet was stolen. Naturally, it didn't start out that way at all—but that's what makes it unexpectedly beautiful.

Somewhere along an otherwise routine day of work as a youth outreach manager in the inner city, my wallet vanished from my office. It was a crushing moment when I discovered it was all gone: my cash and cheques, identification, membership cards, and the nostalgia of the wallet itself, which was one of my only souvenirs from the year I lived in Southeast Asia. But that sinking feeling deepened when the double whammy hit me that one of my clients had stolen it straight from my purse.

Ouch.

The frenzy of cancelling all my accounts and tracking down new ID was almost as agonizing as the panic of counting down the minutes before I had to drive to the airport to pick up an out-of-country friend who had never been to Canada before. Wallowing home in a bubble of self-pity with a temporary client card after a tedious visit to the bank, I tried to mentally prioritize the rest of my professional tasks for the day while also squeezing in my personal responsibilities—like filing a police report and getting my apartment ready for my international guest, to name a few. With a deflated spirit, I made a few quick phone calls to tell the people I most loved that I was having a hard day and could use all the prayers and good vibes they could spare.

All it took was an hour. Within sixty minutes of reaching out to a few family members and friends, the beauty of my situation was awakened.

My brother-in-law immediately made a series of phone calls to find the closest agency in my vicinity to acquire my ID and lent me his Jeep to take care of my errands. My boyfriend, who lived in another province, was prepared to hop into his car and drive six hundred kilometres just to give me a bear hug and reassure me that he was there to support me. Both of my parents were on standby next to the phone in case I called, meanwhile strategizing on the quickest way they could wire me the sum of money that had disappeared with the rest of my wallet. Meanwhile, my sister broke into my apartment with a medley of cleaning supplies and scrubbed away until my place was dazzlingly guest-worthy for my friend's imminent arrival. And although I didn't know it at the time, when a friend of mine back in Cambodia found out about the theft, she bought me an identical wallet from the same lady I'd purchased my original one from and delivered it in person during a break from the field.

With the assemblage of some of the most treasured people in my life rallying around me, my bad day started showing traces of beauty, of love, of comfort, of joy.

Listening for the beautiful in the beastly, for the calm in the chaos, for the virtuous in the vile isn't as automatic as withdrawing money from an ATM. It's not a sensate perception. We weren't created with a receptor to detect the good among the bad in the same way that we were created to perceive taste, sight, smell, touch, and sound. There's nothing natural about it. It's an active choice.

Finding good in the presence of evil is challenging simply because evil has a cunning way of doing all it can to silence the melodies of beauty. Evil is hard-wired to besiege hope and then destroy it. It is programmed to breed wherever we have allowed discouragement and resentment to take root. It seeks to isolate and belittle and disempower. Evil desires to distract us from the simple gifts of whimsy and humour and the sacredness of community because it is these very things that help us to survive and fight back.

In my work as a justice advocate, I often struggle to locate the pockets of goodness in my day. Spending my time with an inner-city youth who was born into an abusive family and channels her desire to find belonging through gang membership gives scant credence to the possibility that she will ever live a "normal" life. Working in rural villages with the highest rates of human trafficking globally is an inauspicious place to find hope when I hear disturbing accounts of forced labour and child exploitation more often than stories of success and freedom.

Sometimes I trudge through weeks of crises with clients before I hear a case with the slightest glimmer of encouragement. But it is never about quantity—it *can't* be about quantity. I cannot define my vocation by the amount of pain or by the frequency of catastrophe. I cannot allow myself to be discouraged by the tribulations, even if they comprise the majority of my day, because the good I encounter has incalculable value.

Weeks passed by, and my stolen wallet never showed up. But the beauty of my situation did. It materialized in the calming reprieve of my loved ones' support. In the sweet solidarity of being reminded that even though conflict is inevitable, I never have to struggle alone. In listening for the beautiful—in learning to hold on to it and never let go.

No, the point isn't to ignore the bad. We need to address it, accept it, and deal with it because even the bad contains value of its own kind.

The point isn't to pit the good against the bad either, because neither can be measured. Would I try to compare the joy of experiencing the respite of the first hot day of summer with the ache of the coldest night of winter? Would it make any sense for me to juxtapose the beauty of a newborn baby with the grief of losing a grandparent when both are profound emotional experiences?

It's not about polarity—it's about integration. It's about learning to accept both, acknowledge value in each, and realize that perhaps the infrequency of the good isn't proportionate to its benefit.

So I Stayed

My calling led me and compelled me to stay in a line of work where hope and goodness are scarce. Modern-day slavery is worse today than it ever was during the transatlantic slave trade over two hundred years ago. Some say as many as thirty-six million people are forced to work against their will, from factories to brothels, restaurants to strip clubs, in practically every country across the world—even in my own backyard in Canada.

Where is hope in something so evil and overwhelming? How do I hope things will get better when the problem only seems to get bigger?

In dark times like these, hope is a tough pill to swallow. Especially when it comes to something as egregious as human trafficking, I struggle to tell myself the usual platitudes of "Stay positive … Stick with it … It will get better." I'm getting a little tired of hearing the trite cliché "But there is hope!" at the end of a lecture about the millions of children forced to work against their will around the world or about the billions of dollars that slavery generates every year.

So why do I stay? Why do I continue to get up in the morning, knowing I'm likely get beaten down again?

Because I know the ugliness of fighting against injustice is not the whole story.

Because I can't experience the good without also experiencing the bad. They coincide. They overlap just as much as joy and despair, peace and pain, victory and tragedy. We know hope because we know disappointment. And we choose hope because it reminds us why we need to keep going.

Because I believe that, despite all the bad, there is still goodness to protect. I want to bring beauty into the world because I believe the world was created to be beautiful. I want to work for justice because I believe the world was made to be just. And in all of this, I believe the words a survivor of trafficking once said as she stood up before an entire court in the Midwest and declared with confidence, "Just because you feel helpless doesn't mean it's hopeless."

Because no matter how dark things get, no matter how hard the work becomes, it can never compare to the beauty that emerges in the most unexpected but profound ways.

Most of all, I choose to stay because even if the final outcome isn't good or even fair, isn't what I wanted or expected, it's okay to feel that discouragement. It's okay to know what it's like to taste defeat or feel overwhelmed or know bitterness, because maybe that's exactly what leads me to something more, to something better.

Maybe it leads me to a new path, to broader growth, to deeper understanding. Maybe it takes me beyond what I desire to what I *really* need. Maybe I can still move forward in faith, even if I can't see the healing or renewal coming.

PART III

LIVING BEAUTIFULLY

Remember one thing:
that you should not leave this earth
unless you have made it a little more beautiful,
a little lovelier,
a little more loving.
—Osho

CHAPTER 13

Walking in Humble Imperfection: Embracing Failure

I err, therefore I am.
—Saint Augustine

Stepping off an international flight with hopeful reverie, I walked through the doors to the international arrivals area in total oblivion to the imminent catastrophe waiting for me.

After being in a long-distance relationship for the past six months, I was finally about to be reunited with my boyfriend for fourteen blissful days. As an ardent perfectionist, I'd prepared myself to win over his family and maybe even walk away with their blessing for our future engagement. It was going to be a perfect two weeks—it *had* to. Because, all my life, striving for perfection had been the only thing I'd known.

The problem with growing up with perfection as the ultimate and only standard is how much more mortifying, how much more crippling that inevitable experience of failure is when it finally comes. More or less, I'd managed to make it through life virtually unscathed until three weeks after my twenty-third birthday, when my coming-of-age moment of failure finally detonated—and at the worst possible time.

After seizing the suitcase I'd been living out of for the past wayfaring year from the luggage carousel, I scoured the baggage claim area impatiently for my boyfriend. When I finally spotted him walking toward me with a goofy grin on his face, I was surprised to see he wasn't alone—his doting mother had accompanied him to pick me up at the airport too. I hadn't seen this man in about two hundred days, yet his mom budged her way in front of him and claimed the first hug, flinging her arms around me with a suffocating squeeze. It was as if his mother intuitively sensed I was someone she wanted to hold on to in more than a literal sense.

I met not only his parents in the two weeks he and I spent together but the *whole* crew: his clan of siblings, including their spouses and children; his friends and church family; even both sets of grandparents. Although it should have been a terribly intimidating event—especially for me as a compulsive people pleaser—it turned out to be a welcoming experience of unconditional fellowship. His mom affectionately spoiled me like a revered out-of-town guest while also treating me as if I'd been a member of the family for years. His siblings adopted me as one of their own, even embracing my offbeat sense of humour and quirky Canadian mannerisms.

The highlight, though, was sharing two mellow weeks with the man I wanted to spend the rest of my life with. Beyond bonding over family gatherings, he and I grew even closer during humid afternoons spent kayaking on the ocean, slurping thick vanilla milkshakes at used bookstores, and exploring seaside markets and hipster cafés. We caught each other up on soul-revealing conversations along the stony beach near the house he grew up in and dreamt out loud about the different capacities we wanted our humanitarian work to take. We swapped music recommendations from new bands we'd discovered during our six months apart and laughed until our bellies hurt from our shared irreverent sense of humour.

Part of me was caught up in the joy of finally seeing him after half a year apart. The other part of me was distracted by the abstractions of our future. Although we both revelled in those cherished carpe diem moments of spending quality time together, we also knew we needed to broach that consequential topic of where to go from here. We didn't want to remain in an international long-distance relationship forever. It was too hard struggling with the frustration of chronically poor Internet connections, living in different time zones, and agonizing over the months of time before we'd see each other again. Given that we'd talked about marriage numerous times before, I figured it was only a matter of time before one of us would break down and move to be with the other.

At the pinnacle of our treasured reunion in our final twenty-four hours together, we took a stroll through the quiet streets of the neighbourhood he grew up in to have that anticipated conversation. Before the end of our walk, he had ended our relationship.

And I was crushed.

In painfully slow motion, I still remember the loss of breath as he quickly spilled all the reasons why our relationship couldn't work out after all. His rationale was too much for me to process in the moment, so all I could do was hold myself together until I had a moment alone on the stony beach to crumble into pieces. To me, it wasn't just a breakup. It was a failure—on *my* part.

One of the worst parts of this soul-crushing perceived failure was that it came with little opportunity to process it in seclusion. Since I still had a full day with him *and* his family before I flew back home, it became twenty-four hours of awkward humiliation as we reluctantly honoured commitments for sociable outings with his family. Pathetically, I tried to wear a composed veneer as if I hadn't just had my heart broken—but I wasn't truly present. I remained a passive participant in that final day together: there only in physical presence, masked by a shadow of wordless devastation.

After enduring the most demoralizing day of my life at that point, we woke up the following morning in a haze of gloominess and half-heartedly joined some of his family and friends for brunch. I positioned myself as far away from him at the table as possible, put on an falsely upbeat spirit, and refused to let anybody know my heart had stopped beating.

Climbing into the passenger seat of his truck after brunch, I maintained that steely exterior as he drove me to the airport. We sat in piercing silence, except for the radio static and the haunting lyrics about having faith even when healing never seems to come.

Silently, he got out of the truck after parking curbside at international departures and dropped my weathered suitcase off on the sidewalk. Hands crammed into the front pockets of his well-worn jeans, he looked sadly into my eyes and for a moment, I wondered if he was hurting as much as I was. His sombre expression evoked just enough mercy within me to dismantle the temptation to punish him by walking away without a word, so I let him give me one last lingering hug before we parted ways for good.

Not for a moment did I let him see how completely deflated I was by the lack of closure and, even more burdensome, the pain of failing to be enough.

Embracing Imperfection

From the time I first entered the public school system, I quickly learned as a student that there is a stark worth-defining, merit-assigning differentiation between succeeding and failing. Through A-pluses, *Well Done!* scratch-and-sniff stickers, and offhand verbal praise, I was rewarded whenever I was correct. But the scowl of a teacher or the burning red mark of a poor grade told me I was irrefutably and profoundly wrong. There really was no middle ground.

By the time I pursued university and a full-time career, I had figured out that the best way to get through life was by not making any mistakes at all. I saw how failure could be terminal: how a moment of weakness could end the career of a politician or how quickly one wrong move could render somebody bankrupt. So I opted to try not making any errors in anything I did, because I knew I would otherwise be subjected to the sting of shame and inadequacy. And, by consigning myself to becoming a chronic perfectionist and an obsessive overachiever, I never fully learned how to handle failure.

In the wake of my devastating breakup, I earnestly believed the demise of our relationship had been a result of my own defects and inadequacies. Haunted by that unconvincing cliché he'd used—"It's not you; it's me"—I spent the better part of a year believing that I was the failure. Meanwhile, I ignored all logic, all realities that we had been going nowhere, all the warning signs from the previous year that our relationship had been parading on a sinking ship for quite a while.

A few weeks passed after that turbulent visit with him and his family, yet I continued to live in blind disbelief that he'd actually let me go. And at such a humiliating time too. Because only two weeks after our mystifying breakup, I was walking down the aisle of a Lutheran church as the maid of honour at my sister's wedding, without him to be my escort. During most of the ceremony and the wedding party photos, the speeches and the dinner and the dance, I kept gazing toward the entrance, waiting for him to change his mind about me and show up.

By the time we sent off the bride and groom on their honeymoon at the end of the night with a benediction of sparklers lighting up the darkened sky, he still hadn't come. He never would come.

To this day, I wish I could transport myself as I am today—knowing what I know now—back in the past to that moment. I would give my heartbroken, confused younger self a hug and insist there is hope in moments like these. That, as Napoleon Hill phrased it, "every adversity, every failure, every heartache carries with it the seed of an equal or greater benefit."

Then, as an encouraging piece of evidence, I would pull out a photograph from my back pocket and show my young, naive self a picture of me taken two years down the road. That picture would depict a very different me—a me with twinkling eyes and a genuine smile worn by someone with unmistakable hope and peace, by someone who refused to let disappointments keep her from joy, by someone who didn't allow her failures to define her but to refine her.

Then I'd pull out another photo to reassure my younger self that things were going to get better. I'd show photos of me doing the very thing I'd never been able to do while in a long-distance relationship: two months of solo backpacking in Eastern Europe. I'd convince my younger self that in just a few months I'd be strolling through the ancient cobblestone streets in Montenegro with nothing but my backpack. I'd be savouring the taste of Turkish coffee in outdoor cafés and buying freshly roasted chestnuts from street vendors in Belgrade. I'd promise my younger self that I would soon start to leave a little bit more of the ache behind while climbing the highest peaks of the Adriatic coast, exploring twenty thousand metres of underground caves in Slovenia, and watching waves crash aggressively into the craggy Croatian seashore from the old walled city of Dubrovnik.

I'd tell my younger self to hang in there—that I'd soon be walking the stone-flanked alleys of vibrant Sarajevo with hopeful reverie, fully mesmerized by the eclectic collision of colours and religions where an Islamic mosque, a Jewish synagogue, a Catholic cathedral, and a Hindu temple coexisted within the same city block. In a matter of time, I'd start developing a renewed sense of freedom while marvelling at the tiny towns hugging medieval castles and the spectacular autumn colours outside the window of a train slowly chugging its way over rolling Bosnian hills wrapped in a carpet of gold and crimson trees. With every new town, new country, new landscape, I'd be reminded it was because of "failure" that these sights were mine.

And, as a voice from the future, I'd tell my broken-hearted self that all the beauty in my life that was about to unfold wouldn't end with that one travelling adventure either. That, in fact, when I came home from my insular trek across Eastern Europe, I'd start dusting off aging aspirations I'd set aside years ago that had always seemed too risky, too prone to failure.

"I know you don't feel hopeful right now," I would tell my younger self that would be quizzically trying to absorb all this information, "and I know it's hard to believe that so much good is going to come out of so much bad. But I promise, it will get better. I know you don't feel brave enough at this moment, but this thing you call 'failure' is going to drive you full tilt into enriching experiences you've never felt courageous enough to pursue. You're going to start ticking items off your life's to-do list. You're going to travel and live all around the world. You're going to write a book. You're going to meet someone new. Not just anybody either—someone who loves you for who you are, flaws and all, without expecting you to be perfect.

"And yes, you're going to have to face more setbacks, but you'll know how to handle them better. They won't quash your dreams and squelch your spirit anymore. If anything, you're going to emerge from these future setbacks with fortified dreams and an amplified spirit. Because this isn't it. This isn't the end. This is the start of something great."

If only. If only I could've sent myself from the future to comfort me at that time. Instead, I had to let time push me along before I could start reawakening old dreams.

Sometime during that year of trying to reconcile the breakup, I received a phone call from a former tree planter whom I had hired and trained a few summers earlier. He had by no means been the strongest tree planter on my crew and had even ended up leaving before the summer was over because he'd felt he wasn't cut out for the work. Now he was calling me to see if I would be an employer reference for his medical school application—not to endorse his skills as an applicant but to vouch for his experience of being humbled by failure. According to the essay section in his application, a successful candidate was someone who knew what it was like to fail and work through the consequences.

I was humoured. But I was also impressed. If a professional discipline as distinguished as medicine could accept and even promote personal failures as a meaningful opportunity for growth, why couldn't the same rule apply to me and my life?

Maybe it did. Maybe I too was allowed to err and fail. Maybe failing didn't even make me a failure. Maybe the mistakes I made and losses I felt didn't have to doom me for life.

It was immediately after that phone call that I began searching for flights online, and I wound up in Eastern Europe a couple of weeks later. And when I came home from that trip, I did allow myself to lean into the other dreams I'd abandoned while I was doing everything I could to keep a hopeless relationship patched together. I took chances by applying for jobs I thought were way out of my league and ended up landing my dream job overseas. I allowed myself the grace to treat myself to spontaneous weekends with friends in New York City and Bangkok—something I'd never felt worthy of doing before. I travelled to places I'd never heard of and lived in parts of the world I never thought I'd get to see. I made lifelong friends scattered along the way. I was challenged and stretched and pushed out of my comfort zone in exhilarating ways.

More than ever, I needed these kinds of wins in the wake of my heartbreak. But there was a dark underbelly to this litany of adventures that I tried to hide from everyone, especially from myself. Because truthfully, my subconscious intention at the time was predicated on the desperate desire to outrun the pangs of loss and the inability to properly grieve. All I wanted was to escape from the crushing humiliation of being dumped when I was expecting a proposal instead.

Travel and adventures and meeting new people helped. But they helped more as painkillers rather than helping to fix the pain itself. I couldn't truly start to heal until I addressed the core of the problem: the fact that, when he and I had been together, I'd never felt I could measure up to his standards. I hadn't been smart enough, spiritual enough, humanitarian enough, or attractive enough. I'd spent the entire trajectory of our relationship trying to hide and fix my imperfections—mostly for his sake. To be perfect for him. No—to be enough for him.

The loss and devastation in the aftermath began to ease when I'd allowed enough time to pass that I could reach a point of acceptance. Because accepting failure didn't have to mean accepting defeat. And once I got to that point, it started feeling like less of a breakup and more of a release. My sadness grew into relief. Because now, without him in my life, I no longer had to be perfect according to someone else's expectation. I could just be me—and I was enough.

And so, in a strange, strange way, failure freed me.

There's Nothing Perfect about Service

The burden of perfectionism becomes a little heavier and a little more complicated when it's moved into a humanitarian context. For me, that struggle became very real when I realized that inferiority complexes were a systemic issue in almost every single non-profit organization I'd worked for. It was never enough to be ordinary—to help struggling youth with their homework or to help people with chronic unemployment to find stable work. Especially given the competition between non-profits for the same sources of funding, the expectation was to do *everything* and to do it perfectly.

It reminded me all too much of the unhealthy power imbalance I'd experienced with my former boyfriend, how I'd worked for the sole purpose of pleasing him to my own detriment. Except in this case, it wasn't a boyfriend I was trying to please but public supporters, private donors, and my staff. And instead of striving for the approval of a mate, I now needed to perform alongside a team with enough excellence to secure the financial resources that would allow our organization to provide life-giving services to the people who needed it most.

Pressuring non-profits to be perfect creates an interesting paradox because, in addition to the demands of perfection, non-profits are also expected to be transparent and accountable. We don't let them make mistakes, but we also don't let them be anything but 100 percent honest about every detail of their spending and programming, their statistics and degree of impact. And maybe that's why so many non-profits embellish their stories, sensationalize the trials experienced by their clients, and bury their mistakes from the public eye: because while the option of choosing either perfection or humility is a tough decision, the former looks a lot more appealing.

And this is troubling—because there's nothing perfect about service.

What's equally disconcerting is that so much work is left undone when we don't feel equipped in all the right ways to take it on. We feel as if we need a special anointing in order to be helpers. That's how perfectionism works: if we can't do something flawlessly, then we'd rather not do it at all.

We're doing a major disservice to justice, however, if we believe we need to be perfect before we can volunteer to mentor a local at-risk youth in our community or sign up to serve with a medical mission overseas. As my friend Kaitlyn has said to me with piercing honesty before, "I don't think God expects us to have life fully put together in order to help people."

Justice, as far as I've seen, has only ever been sought by imperfect people with messy lives, by people who accept that they are more than their inadequacies and who choose to serve in spite of them. Some of the most effective humanitarians I've seen are people who know that their human flaws aren't obstacles to seeking justice—that, if anything, our flaws help bring us closer to the sorrows and joys of others. Who is in a better position to serve alongside people in brokenness than someone who knows what it is to be broken?

For people in want or need of help, there is nothing more encouraging than knowing the person helping them on their feet has fallen before too. In our own time of need, most of us would prefer someone who meets us on our level rather than someone who puts on an air of infallibility and moral supremacy.

It isn't our perfections that qualify us to work for justice, but our humanity.

On a broader scale, non-profits as a whole need to stop hiding behind a guise of faultlessness and start coming clean about what seeking justice really looks like. Some of them have already started to do this. Ashoka, a social entrepreneurship non-profit, suggests that international development cannot be pursued without a certain level of boldness and even risk taking.[1] Engineers Without Borders has cleverly produced an annual *Failure Report* to showcase the projects and strategies that didn't turn out exactly as expected.[2]

Other non-profits are publicly admitting their mistakes through online outlets such as www.AdmittingFailure.org. These are organizations that know how difficult it is to explain to donors that their funding was funnelled into a project that didn't survive the year, but they also recognize that taking calculated risks are a better alternative than being prohibitively frugal with innovation and restrictive of creativity. Agencies like this need to become more of the norm rather than the exception.

As much as I don't want to see the institutions we uphold fail, I also want them to be honest and relatable when they do. I want them to thrive in spite of their mistakes. And I want the same thing for the people in my life—and for myself too.

Is Failure Worth It?

I hate failure. I really do. But sometimes it's the only catalyst that can push me far enough out of my comfort zone to finally do the things I've always wanted to do. Sometimes it is the only thing that breaks me down enough to challenge the way I've been living and to push me in a new direction.

A couple of years ago, I had the pleasure of hearing Brené Brown, a social work professional and researcher on vulnerability, speak at a conference. She asked a question I can never forget: "What is worth doing even if you fail?"

It takes great vulnerability to love somebody, to take a chance on a long-distance relationship, even if the relationship is never guaranteed to last. It takes a lot of courage to champion justice, especially when injustice only seems to worsen and our efforts sometimes seem insignificant. It takes unrelenting audacity to dream—and keep dreaming—when meeting our goals is still a long way off. But isn't all that worth trying anyhow?

Embracing failure isn't about giving up or giving in. It's about rising above our mistakes and unmet expectations with dignity. It's about doing so without shame or depletion, without confusing our failures with our identity and worthiness.

Failure isn't fatal. Failure is not only inevitable but also potentially fruitful. Maybe failure isn't only to be tolerated but is also to be embraced as vital to creativity, innovation, and progress.

If justice is dichotomized as having outcomes of either success or failure, then we are setting ourselves up for disappointment. Martin Luther King Jr. was assassinated while still fighting for civil rights, but I've never heard anybody criticize him for failing. He believed his cause was worth fighting for, whether or not he lived to see the final outcome.

How might life be different if I chose to live like him every day? How much more energy would I have left over to pick myself up from my fall if I didn't expend all my energy on trying not to fall in the first place? How much bigger could I dream for the non-profit I work for if I wasn't afraid of letting my boss down or disappointing our supporters?

I'm trying to accept the inevitability of failure, knowing that—ironically enough—it can conceive new possibilities and is the birthplace of meaningful change. Because even if my most intrepid aspirations do not flourish into success and perfection as I imagine they will, I can remember that there are some things that are always worth pursuing—even if I fail.

---

[1]   David Bornstein, How to Change the World: Social Entrepreneurs and the Power of New Ideas (New York: Oxford University Press, 2007).

[2]   "Admitting Failure," Engineers Without Borders, 2011, http://www.ewb.ca/ideas/admitting-failure-0

CHAPTER 14

Living Abundantly:
With an Attitude of Gratitude

When I arise in the morning,
I'm torn between the desire to improve
the world and to enjoy the world.
This makes it difficult to plan my day.
—E. B. White

There's a stretch of road between Bangkok and the seedy Thai-Cambodian border city of Poipet that always sent me—and perhaps numerous foreign travellers before me—into an existential dilemma.

Along the three-hour journey, the road begs a series of questions for the pondering soul: *How does beauty coexist with depravity? How can so much affluence and abject poverty dwell in the exact same place? And how am I supposed to strike the balance between joy and sadness, between indulgence and self-punishment?*

On my first trip, I prepared to travel this route with a friend on a week's break from my less-than-upbeat counter-trafficking work in Poipet, unaware of the perplexing paradox I was about to encounter. On the morning of our departure, my friend and I wrestled our way through a throng of noisy tuk tuk drivers and land-mine survivors begging for money as we crossed the Thai border on foot. Barefoot children hustled from tourist to tourist with outstretched palms, using whatever English they knew to ask for spare change. Young, beautiful women in short skirts with faces painted heavily with makeup disappeared into Poipet's version of the Bermuda Triangle: a strip of casinos and nightclubs that swallowed them up, never to spit them out again.

Once we boarded the bus and began travelling westward, every inch of ground closer to Bangkok indicated we were entering a brand-new world. Roads became smoother, and the buildings grew taller and taller. A white line suddenly appeared down the middle of the road, dividing traffic in a strangely orderly way.

Living in the chaotic conditions of Cambodia, I'd grown accustomed to roads being the unregulated domain of noisy motorbikes transporting stacks of pigs to the market while also being used to discard beer cans, diapers, and other trash. As we rolled into the outskirts of the commercialized metropolis of Bangkok, I was shocked to see roads functioning for the purpose of commuting, not as an alternative to a garbage dump. With my nose pressed against the dusty glass of the window, I tried to fully take in the wonders of the land of plenty: its traffic lights, its five-storey malls, its well-paved roads with organized systems to control traffic.

I was awestruck by the contrast in the human dynamics too. Instead of donning themselves in flannel Angry Birds pyjamas and second-hand flip-flops as Cambodian women often did, many of the women I saw in Bangkok wore neatly pressed dresses and high heels and styled their hair at high-end, air-conditioned salons. Instead of motorcycle taxi drivers draining cans of beer all day as they often did in Poipet, my first Thai taxi driver politely addressed me in articulate English and immediately engaged me in a knowledgeable conversation about climate change and Greenpeace.

I struggled to process the stark contrasts between my life in Cambodia and my first visit to Thailand. I was astonished that a middle class existed in Bangkok, where it wasn't only wealthy expats or tourists who enjoyed a decent quality of life but locals too. Here, average Thais indulged in meals at fancy restaurants that abided by health codes. They leisurely strolled through well-manicured parks with their families and sat quietly on a Sunday afternoon with a newspaper in Starbucks (yes—*Starbucks!*).

Stepping temporarily away from the gritty life I lived in Cambodia and into the luxuries offered by Bangkok, I was terribly uncomfortable. Was it okay to delight in taking hot showers and having a reliable water supply at my hotel, knowing that, back at home, only a little over half of Cambodians had access to safe water? Was it wrong to enjoy air-conditioned movie theatres and malls and coffee shops when the people I served back in Poipet slept in the unrelenting heat in open-air bamboo huts?

Secretly, I envied the Westerners who came to travel the beaches and urban areas of Thailand, incognisant of the level of poverty that existed outside of the tourist hotspots highlighted in their Lonely Planet guidebooks. They seemed so content in their ignorance, so peaceful in their oblivion.

Meanwhile, I was overwhelmed by guilt every time I turned on a faucet spouting warm water or regaled in the novelty of a frothy latté at Starbucks.

On our last evening in Bangkok, my friends and I planned an opulent evening together, cruising across the Chao Phraya River to an exclusive-feeling island for a fancy dinner. With wide-eyed approval at the options on the menu, we all ordered food we knew would be only a distant memory once we returned to Cambodia. We swayed to the live music playing softly in the background and reminisced about our highlights from our time in Bangkok.

Beneath the surface, though, all I could picture was the weathered face of the single mom I always saw wandering the darkened streets in Phnom Penh, searching for discarded edibles for her two young children to get through the night.

I was torn. Torn between gratification and guilt. Torn between wanting to enjoy the simple pleasures of life and wondering if it was wrong for me to do so.

An Ethical Tug-of-War

Living an examined life has been both freeing and disempowering for me. As a child, I began learning the world was both a magical and misguided place. Then I started seeing contrasts of both beauty and brokenness in my travels as an adult. Eventually I started experiencing the interminable pull between joy and sorrow in my work as a humanitarian, which has made my life a tug-of-war between wanting to fix the world and wanting to enjoy it.

At the start of my humanitarian endeavours, the thought of being able to enjoy the world seemed impossible to me. I thought my job was to punish myself for not being part of the one billion people living on less than a dollar a day or for not belonging to the 40 percent of individuals without access to basic sanitation.[1] And being anaesthetized with a heavy dose of white guilt, I thought I had a personal responsibility for reversing these kinds of statistics.

As a young, recent university graduate and a small-town Prairie girl, I launched my vocation with a jarring move to a desolate city in rural Mexico, too naive and inexperienced to know how to handle the poverty I was seeing. I struggled to reconcile my litany of unearned privileges with the cramped houses made of garbage bags and sticks, the barefoot children scavenging for food in the city dump, the bruises we found on our students, and the stories of neglect and violence they brought with them to school every day. Quickly, I became a walking time bomb, about to explode from the building pressure of unresolved guilt.

Inconveniently enough, my time ran out at Christmas—and so did my work contract. After a heartbreaking goodbye to all my students, I flew home to Canada resentfully with a sullen attitude. There, self-punishment quickly lost its productive value. I spent the entire holidays moping around the house, shooting daggers at the festively decorated Christmas tree as if my cold glares could hurt its feelings. At Christmas Eve dinner, I joined my family at the table only in presence, declaring that I was on a hunger strike. "If my kids in Mexico aren't eating Christmas dinner right now," I announced bitterly, "then neither will I!"

Even under the auspices of my loving parents, I felt isolated. I thought I'd never fit back into mainstream life in the developed world. On the one hand, I knew I wasn't alone in my struggle to reintegrate after years of overseas humanitarian work. I knew a relief worker in Liberia who had thrown up in the dental-care aisle at a drugstore in his hometown in Michigan because he'd been dizzy from too many options of toothpaste to choose from. A Canadian friend who had served in China had clocked a three-year recovery period before she could feel functional at home again. I knew it was normal to experience reverse culture shock and to feel lost in the re-entry process. Yet this solidarity had little comfort to me as I wondered if I'd ever feel joy again.

All I'd known of my justice advocacy was watching suffering and experiencing suffering, either vicariously or personally. In order to continue qualifying as a humanitarian in Canada, I thought I had to renounce everything: from the small, material luxuries of middle-class living to withdrawing from the people I loved the most. With every cup of coffee I shared with old friends or every time I accidentally ran into an acquaintance at the bank or grocery store, I felt like a phony. They all spoke the usual platitudes about a sensationalized version of humanitarianism, praising my work as if it were a noble feat.

They believed I had a heart of gold. What I really carried was a heart of guilt.

Suffering for the Cause

After that bitter Christmas visit following my service in Mexico, I began understanding what Oliver Wendell Holmes Jr. meant when he said, "A mind that is stretched by a new experience can never go back to its old dimensions."

For me, there was no going back to a normal, nine-to-five, work-to-live, traditional lifestyle—even though that seemed to come with fewer demands and less emotional distress. Even though it was a little more appealing to live in a self-fulfilled, blissfully unaware Willy Wonka world. Even though it would probably be easier to be ignorant of the realities of a world crumbling from compassion withheld and justice deferred.

I had to keep going. Because donating money to Oxfam or Amnesty International alone was too easy. Because praying for the world's poor from the safety and familiarity of a church pew was not enough.

I did keep going, but mostly because I thought I had no other option. Humanitarians, in my experience, weren't allowed to have it both ways: to have well-balanced, decent lives while serving the most-marginalized and most-desperate of people. And so I beat myself up for choosing this path, feeling quite convinced that I needed to thoroughly suffer the consequences of my own decision.

Wanting to give, wanting to work for justice, wanting something deeper from a traditional Western lifestyle isn't a bad thing. Displacing those emotions is the problem. Never will I be genuinely happy while under the command of a martyr complex, armed with an attitude of masochism, marching to the beat of a cynic's drum.

Yes, I had to keep going, but in a new direction where I couldn't let my guilt control me. Because expecting unwavering perfection and absolute devotion was demanding to a harmful level. Regularly sacrificing my sleep, my health, and my sanity was too much. Pressing forward relentlessly, far out of my comfort zone, thousands of miles away from home—it still had to come with some boundaries.

This didn't become clear to me until I hit my rock bottom years later, when something frightening started happening to me during my service in Cambodia. It wasn't the bombings and civil unrest, the venomous spiders creeping in my bedroom, or the predators trying to break into my house—although those things were frightening in their own way. What alarmed me the most was the realization I was losing my ability to dream.

My wild imagination as a child had continued to cultivate the visions and dreams for my life even as a student studying justice—but then slowly had faded when justice first became my profession. I left Cambodia a lifeless shell of a person, unsure of who I was anymore. No longer an idealist, no longer a dreamer, I returned home to Canada with the regrettable belief that I was forever devoid of a part of me I had always thought to be indivisible from my core.

In retrospect, my dreams hadn't vanished completely. They had been eclipsed by my belief that I had abdicated my right to dream the moment I'd committed my life to serving others. Now, the task was to unlearn that belief and to allow room for my dreams once more.

Abundant Living

After a year of serving in Cambodia, I went through the re-integration process once again. But this time, I had travelled farther, stayed longer, and hurt more than I ever had before. I'd seen exploited migrant workers being transported as chattel in caged vehicles on a daily basis. I'd seen land-mine survivors without any limbs begging for pennies and malnourished children lifting heavy loads for the production of cassava and rubber. I'd seen how a country could still be crushed after being scourged by genocide decades earlier—only to crumble once again under the authority of a violent dictator who was complacent toward the suffering of his people.

One of the hardest things an overseas humanitarian goes through doesn't always happen in his or her country of assignment. Sometimes the hardest thing is coming back home, because starting over is hard. Time doesn't stand still back at home just because you weren't there to take it all in. Friends change. Babies are born, and grandparents age. New technology replaces the old. Nothing is the same anymore.

Yet for me, the hardest part of coming home is often figuring out how to straddle that gap between the basic, even deprived life I once had overseas with the privileges and comforts of being back at home. Early on, as I first eased my way into a humanitarian circle, I saw how having the fewest material possessions possible warranted bragging rights. Living primitive lives in dangerous countries, we believed our puritanical ways were right and that the consumer-driven Western lifestyle we'd left behind was wrong. We thought that not having iPhones and travelling by rickshaw somehow made us morally superior.

We looked down upon fellow humanitarians who moved back home, because to us it meant they were selling out.

In all this, I braced myself for a sloppy and painful re-entry as I returned to Canada with more baggage than when I'd left. But it was different this time. Naturally, I had plenty of difficult mental and emotional adjustments, in addition to the eighty-degree-Celsius change in temperature. Yet in those initial days, as I wandered around my house with five layers of wool clothing and a blanket wrapped around me at all times, I knew I couldn't feel guilty for the luxury of central heating or owning multiple sets of clothes. Because this time, I'd returned with a new vow to myself: to never regress to empty, resentful, meaningless martyrdom as a coping mechanism. Ever again.

In the weeks to come, I didn't find myself crippled with shame for having hot, running water or reliable electricity. I wasn't self-reproaching at every trendy restaurant or coffee shop I went to with a friend. Instead, I carefully but deliberately leaned into a lifestyle where I was comfortable without being *too* comfortable, where I had every need met without having too much, where I could be at peace without forgetting where I'd come from.

The difference between this reintegration process from any other was finally being able to discriminate between identifying with someone's pain and feeling responsible for it. At the outset of my journey, I'd felt so sorrowful for people's suffering that I had begun helping from a place of guilt. And yet, throughout my travels, I've often encountered people in destitute circumstances who felt less burdened by their situation than I did.

Ironically, some of the biggest hearts, the most-sincere gratitude, and the deepest joy has belonged to the most-resource-poor people I've met. I treasure the memory of a beautiful nine-year-old Mexican girl living in a crowded migrant camp with a vivacious smile stretching across her dirt-smudged face. She shared a precious bag of *churritos* with me as I gave her a piggyback ride around the camp. Her biggest concern wasn't when she'd get her next meal or the cramped conditions of the one-room, tin house her family shared with her grandparents. She just wanted to play and to share the little she had with others.

In my travels in rural Hungary, some of the poorest families in the Romany villages I visited graciously invited my sister and me for elaborate feasts they probably couldn't afford, bringing out their best hand-stitched tablecloths for the occasion. It was similar in Southeast Asia. Every time I made a home visit to a family living in a one-room bamboo hut, they would generously serve me a canned soft drink and fresh fruit that likely cost them more than they could spare. As I was welcomed into their homes and caught a glimpse of their lives, I could see that poverty influenced their lives, but it didn't defeat them.

What separated us wasn't resources or wealth or education or the lavish luxuries of a Western lifestyle. It was gratitude. While I resented the life I was born into, they were grateful for the little they had. While I felt encumbered by injustice and immobilized by despair, they celebrated the gift of life. These were people who understood something that my humanitarian friends and I couldn't: they understood the difference between wealth and abundance. Their happiness wasn't held captive by empty material or circumstantial forces. Although they were poor in resources, they lived in abundant joy and gratitude, in deep spiritual richness, with a wealth of peace and perspective.

And so I had to learn to be happy for their happiness, even though I didn't understand it. Most of all, I had to learn to live my own life in gratitude, as unnatural as it seemed, because gratitude was a far better motivator than guilt ever was.

Trying to apply these lessons I'd absorbed overseas was challenging. My only frame of reference of living minimalistically and as self-sustainably as possible in a Western context was living out of a tent as a tree planter. And truthfully, that had been one of the happiest seasons of my life. Everything I'd needed to survive had been stored in a Rubbermaid container in my generally-but-not-guaranteed waterproof house made of nylon and polyester. It hadn't bothered me that my shower had consisted of tin walls and a garden hose that pumped cold water from a creek or that I'd constantly had a layer of dirt caked onto my face in an unsightly and unfeminine way. My life had been uncomplicated—and I had thrived.

In harsh circumstances, I'd discovered a strength I hadn't known I possessed. I'd found out I could endure a range of austere elements, from sub-zero temperatures with six inches of snow to swelteringly hot summers to three straight weeks of flooding. I'd derived a childlike joy in the simplicity of homemade chocolate-chip cookies and in the gentle, rhythmic strumming of a guitar around a campfire of like-minded twentysomethings. I'd loved having nothing more than laughter and fellowship to get me through the toughest days. It had been all I needed.

But after three consecutive summers of living out of a tent, I'd come to an important conclusion: as peaceful and enjoyable as a bare-bones lifestyle was, it wasn't something I wanted to sustain for the rest of my life. As much as I loved it, the thought of *not* having to bail myself out with a water bottle every time it flooded had become drastically appealing toward the end of my last summer.

Living aesthetically may work well for Buddhist monks and Amish communities, but I had trouble sustaining it in the long term. Denying ourselves the modern conveniences of Western life may be the hallmark of humanitarian ego, but I find that only works in a certain context. Instead, I've resigned myself to living simply: enjoying the small pleasures and moments of simple abundance.

Life looks a little different for me these days. I live in a one-bedroom apartment in downtown Winnipeg that has everything I need and more. I'm still working to prevent human trafficking, but most of my humanitarian friends overseas would question if it's really possible to seek justice while having a comfortable lifestyle. I think it is. Time and experience are showing me that simple living is a state of being, not just a circumstance. It's about deliberately seeking out ways to incorporate a more ethical and environmentally sustainable lifestyle in any given situation—whether we're living in a tent, in a twenty-foot trailer, or in a cosmopolitan city centre. Simple living is a frame of mind.

There is nothing inherently wrong with living comfortably. It's when we put our resources to good use—whether it's finances, intellect, or time—that we begin to give value and purpose to a life of privilege. It's less about how much money we have and more about how we use it that counts. It's less about feeling guilty about the blessings we have and more about how we use those blessings to help others.

Finding Myself Again

Justice motivated me to begin my vocation. Guilt, for a time, was an underlying part of why I stayed. And persistent self-punishment was what brought me to the crossroads of wondering if I could ever enjoy the world or if I would only want to solve its problems.

Maybe there is a moral responsibility for those in positions of power and privilege to do something about injustice. But that can't mean exhausting ourselves over the mission; otherwise, we'll do more harm than good. For me, helping became harmful when I fuelled myself from the wrong energy source, as if I'd filled my car with diesel. Helping didn't hurt as much when I served from a place of gratitude. In fact, it gave far more vitality to my work and well-being than guilt ever did.

Most of all, one of the best ways I've put my misguided life into perspective is by abiding by the words of Howard Thurman: "Do not ask what the world needs. Ask instead what makes you come alive and go do it. Because what the world needs is for more people to come alive."

What makes me come alive is certainly my passion for justice. But it's more than that. It's also cherishing the time I spend with my family. It's the ease of transition between deep conversations to uncontrollable laughter and back again with my closest friends over a cup of coffee. It's working on a creative project set to my favourite playlist. It's the thrill of spontaneous road trips, blazing campfires, and backpacking adventures. It's the simple joys of writing on an outdoor patio or paddling a canoe across a still lake. It's creating and exploring, learning and growing, loving and living.

Justice may be integral to who I am and how I live my life. Yet it's one part of my vocation—a piece belonging to a whole. My vocation is the sum of all the joys and dreams, people and places, and convictions and aspirations that make me come alive. It's more than what I do—it's who I am.

Today, I tend to live on a continuum somewhere along the road between Bangkok and Poipet. There are days when I am caught in the dusty, chaotic swarm of life in Poipet, where my eyes are focused on the systemic problems, on the unmet needs, on the rights that have been breached. Other days, I feel a little closer to paradise—leaning into grace and enjoying the simple pleasures of life, as I did on my first trip to Thailand. And then there are days when I am trapped somewhere in between the two, conflicted between wanting to fix the world while also wanting to enjoy it.

On the days when I resort to guilt, I need to remind myself that making a place for my own happiness is not horribly selfish—that there is actually more harm than helpfulness in running on empty in order to make the world a better place.

The truth is, being a wholehearted person can help to make the world a better place.

---

[1]   UN, "Fast Facts: The Faces of Poverty," Millennium Project, 2006, http://www.unmillenniumproject.org/documents/3-MP-PovertyFacts-E.pdf.

CHAPTER 15

Grief without Despair: Light in the Darkness

> Be soft. Do not let the world [harden your
> heart]. Do not let pain make you hate.
> Do not let the bitterness steal your sweetness. Take
> pride that even though the rest of the world may
> disagree, you still believe it to be a beautiful place.
> —Iain Thomas, "The Fur"

Buried in a valley surrounded by a mountain range swathed in trees lies a small slum at the edge of a sleepy Bulgarian town. The dividing boundary between the slum and the town is uncomfortably blunt, cut along a line of racial discrimination. On the town side, Bulgarians drive motorized vehicles, eat in Westernized restaurants, and live in humble but sturdy houses. Yet on the other side—the slum side—is where the Romany population is expected to live, and they do so in entirely different conditions.

With the exception of driving horse-drawn carts into the outskirts of the town to haul water, the Romany are otherwise not welcome within the city perimeter. They are refused employment, turned away at restaurants, and treated as a subclass of human beings. Compounded by racism stemming from a thousand years back, the Romany experience a severely high unemployment rate, a high illiteracy rate, and staggeringly low life expectancy. And so they commune together in segregation and try to survive with each other's support as much as they can.

Several co-workers and I visited "the other side of the town" while travelling to monitor some of our organization's anti-trafficking projects based in Europe. As threatening rain clouds formed a darkened canopy above our heads, we walked through the trash-lined dirt streets to meet some of these families and hear their stories. Women washing laundry by hand from buckets in their yards waved to us while chickens and children played at their feet in the dirt. The poverty of the families and houses I saw were as bad as some of the villages I'd frequently seen while living in Cambodia.

Life is bleak here in the Romany ghetto.

The storm clouds broke open, and rain began cascading from them, turning the dirt streets into a muddy basin. As we rushed to find shelter, I noticed a young Romany girl—no more than twelve years old—sitting on a bench outside a decrepit house. Her eyes were vacant, staring at nothing but the heaps of trash outside her home. Even from a distance, I could tell that hope had left her a long time ago.

I couldn't blame her. Girls aren't worth very much in these parts. A family celebrates the birth of a girl not for her intrinsic human value but because she can be sold for the price of a horse when she's older. The vast majority of Romany women never complete their schooling, because they're often forced into arranged marriages by the time they reach puberty.

Due to a lack of awareness, most families don't realize that the vulnerability of these girls who are forced into arranged marriages creates the conditions for human trafficking. Often, as soon as her parents leave, an adolescent "wife" turns into a lucrative business venture, where her "husband" or "in-laws" rent her body out to clients as a child prostitute.[1]

What broke my heart the most was the expression of acceptance I saw on that girl's dirt-encrusted face. She knew life had little to offer her here. She knew that in a year or two she'd be exchanged for the price of a horse or sent away to marry a man much older than herself. She knew that if her parents continued to struggle to feed their family, she would likely be kicked out of her house. And as fearful as that would be, she knew the sobering truth about what happened to young Romany girls living off the streets. To our team, it was what we'd call exploitation. She'd just call it life.

In the span of a short afternoon in the Romany slum, I met a playful group of young children with special needs, most of whom had never been to school before. I met an eighteen-year-old boy who had been kicked out of his home when he was young and had no other option for his survival than to prostitute himself to male and female clients on the streets. But of all the things I saw that day, nothing would haunt my mind more than the memory of a twelve-year-old girl staring hopelessly into the cold abyss of her future.

Hoping in the Hopeless

Along my journey for justice, nothing has brought more darkness into my life than fighting human trafficking.

When I lived in Southeast Asia, modern-day slavery became more than an economic and social problem to me. It became raw and real. When the army came with their tanks and raided the house next door to our office in Cambodia and arrested twenty-seven gang members for selling young local women into the sex trade, human trafficking was no longer an article in the newspaper to me. It was something taking place right underneath my nose.

It became deeply personal as I developed closer relationships with my staff, all of whom were Cambodian nationals—and many of whom had lives that had been marred by exploitation. Whether it was somebody's younger sister, somebody's best friend, somebody's parent, or even themselves who had been exploited, it seemed that human trafficking was imprinted all over the personal histories and families of my co-workers. Sometimes their loved ones had migrated illegally to Thailand for work and would come home with mental illness, brain damage, and a long road of recovery before them. Sometimes they'd never returned at all.

Once it became something I saw every day in Cambodia, human trafficking stopped being a subject I wrote academic papers about. It was no longer a theoretical topic up for discussion at a conference, nor was it the wildly inaccurate and glamorized version portrayed in Hollywood films. It was real. It *is* real. And it's the reality—even a way of life—for millions of people in Cambodia, Bulgaria, Canada, the United States, and beyond.

As I became more integrated into Cambodian culture, it seemed to me that injustice permeated every level of personal, professional, and political life. I saw how intricately embedded corruption was within the government and public services. Like when a little boy from a nearby town died from a venomous snakebite because the hospital refused to offer him a vaccine that was reserved for "VIPs only." Or how men justified violence against women based on the old Cambodian proverb "Men are like gold; women are like cloth." One of the most harrowing stories I heard of this nature was when a local woman barely survived a gruesome act of blatant misogyny at the hands of her husband, an ex–Khmer Rouge soldier, who attempted to electrocute her to death. How does a person counterbalance this kind of normalized evil with the belief in restoration? Or the cycle of relapse and the slow pace of change with the beauty of small but significant wins as we move over the arc that is sustained progress and time? Or the grim realities of a relationally and systemically broken world with the hopeful promise of heaven?

Gradually, I started feeling fed up with trying to understand and fix the problems in other countries. It didn't make sense that I, an English-speaking Westerner, was managing a staff of Cambodian nationals who knew far more about the social, political, and economic issues than I did. It didn't make sense for me to struggle through the few broken sentences I knew in a foreign language, without ever being able to fully communicate or understand what the other party was saying. It didn't make sense to try to help when I didn't actually know where the help needed to go.

After my crash and burn in Cambodia, I moved back to Canada with the intent of focusing on the problems in my own neighbourhood. I began working in the inner city of Winnipeg as an outreach manager at a youth drop-in centre. Speaking my native language and working in a familiar context seemed far more efficient to me.

Although this decision may have made more sense, it didn't make the work any easier. I was back in Canada, but I was still dealing with human trafficking. I still saw hunger and malnourishment in the youth I worked with. I still heard frightening stories of domestic violence on a regular basis. I still had to manage the tension of a government that was cutting social programs instead of hearing the cries of its suffering people. I still knew that people living on Aboriginal reserves outside the city didn't have access to clean water and lived in third-world conditions—in my own country.

It took a little over two months of working in the inner city of Winnipeg before I had my first breakdown. That morning, a young mother had come into our drop-in centre, asking me if I could spare a couple of juice boxes for her adorable, brown-eyed twin toddlers. She had an appointment at the emergency food bank in a few hours but didn't have enough spare change to purchase a couple of twenty-five-cent boxes of apple juice in the meantime.

After handing her some juice boxes and granola bars and wishing her luck, I disappeared into the staff bathroom and burst into tears. I cried for her and any other parent in the inner city who had to humble themselves to beg for food for their children.

While I was at it, I cried for Larry, an older gentleman with tattoos etched on his arms from his teenage years, who had a heart of gold and yet still couldn't land himself a job. I cried for the group of rough-and-tumble teenage boys who would shoot hoops in our gym every Friday at lunch before heading down the block to the soup kitchen—not exactly a typical routine for the average nineteen-year-old boy in Canada.

I cried for the kids in our youth program who were so neglected and desensitized to violence that they had played with knives in the park for fun, until our staff found out. I cried at how hard it had been to temporarily suspend these youth from using our services, because it left them no safe place to hang out. They would just end up playing with knives somewhere else.

I cried and I cried until I had nothing left—no more energy to worry about their fate. I had to believe that the mom's appointment at the food bank would go well, that Larry would find a job, that our youth would somehow make it safely through the weekend. Because how was I supposed to help if I had no hope for them?

You Can't Have It Both Ways

Over one of the last warm weekends of the summer, somebody set fire to the playground at our youth drop-in centre, burning it to the ground. The sight was morbid. Somebody had torched the entire structure, leaving nothing but twisted metal and blackened plastic, melted down into an irreparable heap.

Our staff's morale had been low all summer long to begin with. We didn't feel we were making any progress with our youth. In fact, their behaviour and home lives seemed to be worsening. Gang violence and drug use was on a steady increase, especially without school being in session to distract them.

Almost daily, our staff were responding to crisis situations: calling youth suicide hotlines, reporting runaways, breaking up fights ... But on that Monday morning when our staff came to work in shock at the grim sight, our team spirit couldn't have been lower. To me, the pile of ashes that once had been a playground was a visual representation of our efforts: hopeless, wasted, and dead.

Gazing at the scorched remains of the playground next to me was my co-worker Amy, whose buoyant persona broke the silence when she piped up, "Well, thank goodness. These kids needed an excuse for a new playground!"

One of the hardest things to do as a humanitarian is exactly what Amy was able to do: to accept that it's okay to mourn but that it's also okay to move on. To grieve without being numbed by it. To dare to see the light in the darkness.

It's not easy, because evil inherently wants us to feel too overwhelmed to do anything about it. Evil doesn't want us to be able to find humour in the barren times or to strengthen solidarity as a team during a rough season or—worse yet—to still be able to experience happiness and passion, to be able to enjoy our lives despite the doom and disasters that come with it.

For most of my humanitarian pursuits, especially during my year in Cambodia, I'd convinced myself of exactly what evil wanted me to believe. I completely misappropriated my responsibilities, thinking my job was to commiserate with the suffering of others. I thought joy and peace belonged to a separate sphere that couldn't overlap with service and commitment—and since I'd chosen the latter, I could never experience the former.

"You can't have it both ways," I would silently tell myself every day with a heavy heart as I walked under the beating sun to my office in Cambodia. "You can't live in the light while battling against the darkness." Downtrodden, demoralized, and depleted, I started identifying with Frodo Baggins in J. R. R. Tolkien's *The Lord of the Rings* when he wished that the One Ring had never come to him—that he'd never embarked on his pilgrimage to begin with.

On numerous occasions, I'd catch myself echoing those same aching sentiments of feeling burdened by choosing to surrender my life to a paramount quest. The further I pursued my calling of social justice, the more I experienced a deepened sense of doubt and discouragement. Especially when working in Cambodia, I resented my decision to follow my calling to such far and isolated corners of the earth. I often bemoaned to God, "I wish you had never called me—I wish I'd never travelled down this road to begin with."

Yet in those moments, I heard Gandalf's consoling response to Frodo: "So do all who live to see such times, but that is not for us to decide. All we can do is decide what to do with the time that is given to us."[2]

All we can do is decide how to respond. All that's left for me to choose is how to handle the evil in the world. Evil is a hard thing to run from. It was there in Cambodia, and it was there when I returned home to Canada. All I can do is fight against it while trying to not be immobilized by it.

Frankly, I don't know if it's possible to be immune to the pain that comes with fighting against human trafficking or working with gang-involved youth in the inner city. Some parts of my own humanitarian journey have manifested as bad: compromising my health, jeopardizing my safety, and even destroying some of my relationships. The scars etched into my being are why I sometimes have troubles sleeping at night, why I have days when I'm drained before I even get out of bed, why I'm careful to not just trust anybody or anything.

Light and darkness may be mutually exclusive, but we cannot have one without the other. It is through the bad that we know the good. It is through the good that we can defeat the bad.

My experience has taught me that as much as darkness comes with a life of seeking justice, so does a lot of light. While seeking justice has broken me down in some ways, it has built me up in other ways. I've had trials *and* triumphs, hurt *and* healing— sometimes within the same experience. Yes, I've lost the love of someone I deeply cared about because of the demands of this vocation, but the demise of that relationship ultimately freed me to experience new adventures, new possibilities, new life. Even when I was so burned out from overworking that I couldn't take care of myself, it was at my lowest that I felt the most unconditionally loved by my friends and family, who rallied around me with unwavering support.

The darkness I've seen and the pain I've felt in my humanitarian work has made me stronger, wiser, healthier. I've learned how to advocate for my own needs and to free myself through vulnerability. I've discovered how pointless it is to demand perfection from anyone, including myself.

Strangely enough, I've even seen how the dark times have helped the organizations I've worked for. Every case we learned about human trafficking in Cambodia was disturbing and disheartening, but it also made us smarter in learning how to better combat it. That burned-down playground was a crime, but it was also an opportunity for the kids to get a new playground—and for our team to grow stronger together in our sorrow.

So maybe—just maybe—it *is* possible have it both ways after all.

Finding the Beauty

Is it possible to live ethically without being a martyr? Is there a way to work for justice without being consumed by it? Is it permissible to enjoy blessings without feeling undeserving of them? For so long, I've answered these questions with a resounding no. I've separated joy from my work, believing the two could never coexist.

It's time to stop diametrically opposing joy and service, because I can't easily be a beacon of light to a hurting community if I'm living in darkness. I can't help those with heavy hearts if I, myself, struggle under the burden of guilt and despair. I can't cultivate hope in others if I have none to begin with myself.

I need to give myself permission to have a beautiful life, where joy and service aren't mutual exclusives but are close companions that co-exist in the big and small moments—whether it's as momentous as celebrating with a former prostitute who has been clean for two hundred days or as simple as rewarding an ice cream cone to a student with special needs for going a week without wetting the bed.

My own experience of the dark can help me meet those who are suffering at whatever place they are at. I may not know what it's like to be trafficked or to have a gang as my only safety net, but I do know what it's like to be broken, longing for healing. To be drained and dry, longing for restoration. To be lonely, longing for authentic community. To be lost, longing to be found.

I can identify with their suffering, but I'm more useful to people when I'm not consumed by their suffering. I'm more supportive when I empathize within reason, when I give within boundaries, when I labour within limits. By dwelling in the light, I can give hope and inspiration to those who suffer in darkness.

It's by allowing myself to experience joy, peace, laughter, and contentment that I can fuel my drive to battle injustice, chaos, hurt, and brokenness. Maybe Martin Luther King Jr. was right all along about how "darkness cannot drive out darkness; only light can do that. Hate cannot drive out hate; only love can do that."

Service without Defeat

Reconciling my existence in a world with so much good and so much bad is one of the biggest challenges in my life. And it's mainly because of all the bad in the world that I've devoted my life to seeking justice.

It can be a heartbreaking and disillusioning route. Surviving those moments of darkness means being able to learn how to grieve without despair, to serve without defeat. There is a time for service and sacrifice just as much as there is a time to enjoy the beauty in the world. The ugliness that comes with the life of a justice advocate isn't the whole story, because it's a life filled with burdens *and* beauty, losses *and* liberties.

This calling is not just about trying to counter the bad: fighting evil, standing against racism, intervening in human trafficking. It's also about standing for the good. It's about protecting the beauty that already exists in this world. It's more than being against something; it's about being *for* something: for peace, for equality, for freedom.

And that's the other reason why I've devoted my life to seeking justice: because, as messy as the world is, I also believe it to be a wonderful place. I must allow myself the grace to enjoy the mysteries and majesties and miracles of the world in order to see it as a place worth redeeming.

---

[1] European Roma Rights Centre, Breaking the Silence: A Report by the European Roma Rights Centre and People in Need (Budapest: European Roma Rights Centre and People in Need, 2011), 73.

[2] J. R. R. Tolkien, The Fellowship of the Ring (New York: Houghton Mifflin Company, 1954), 50.

CHAPTER 16

Redemptive Trials: Refined by Fire

Within us all there are wells of thought and dynamos of energy which are not suspected until emergencies arise. Then, often times, we find that it is comparatively simple to double or triple our former capacities and to amaze ourselves by the results.
—Thomas J. Watson

Gusts of wind severed heavy sheets of rain, blowing them erratically and threatening to take down anything left standing. Shivering at the top of the precarious cliff, I gazed at the vast expanse of forest and lakes and mountains barely visible through torrents of rain. The showers saturated my clothes and added extra weight to my already-sagging bags of pine and spruce seedlings strapped to my waist. Longing for shelter and aching from soreness, I wondered how on earth I'd managed to spend my twentieth birthday with such a haphazard misadventure as this.

It was my first summer out in the northern wilderness of British Columbia as a tree planter. Earning ten cents per tree, I had to plant furiously in order to earn enough to pay my daily camp fees, let alone to cover my tuition costs for university in the fall.

And it was backbreaking work. During the first two weeks of the season, we'd lost planters who had either willingly quit or been fired because their foreman had enough mercy to know they wouldn't last more than a few weeks. If you made it through that first month, you were more likely to make it through the summer—that is, if the joint injuries, tumbles down steep cliffs, and grizzlies didn't get you first.

Sometimes, in the stillness of the night, I could hear somebody faintly crying from inside their tent. It happened most frequently on the coldest nights, when temperatures dipped below freezing and it didn't seem to matter how many layers of wool clothes you wore or how thick your sleeping bag was. It was enough to break any man or woman, no matter how physically strong they were.

Tree planting was more of a mental game than a physical challenge. Fortunately, for a woman of average strength and less-than-average athleticism, that meant I still had a chance of surviving. What I lacked in muscles, I made up for in stamina. What I lacked in experience, I compensated with attitude.

And so, at the top of a cliff on the day I turned twenty years old, I knew I needed perseverance to start kicking in. As dwarfed as I was by the treacherous terrain and as insufficient as I felt I was for the task, there was still a piece of land that needed to be reforested—and it was up to me to plant it.

Reluctantly, I began my steep descent, clinging onto roots and shrubs growing out of the cliff with one hand while grasping my shovel in the other. On the bright side, the precipitation restrained the swarms of buzzing mosquitoes and flesh-eating black flies for the moment—but it also made the slippery slope as much of a hazard as the field of stinging nettle and devil's club waiting for me at the bottom. Every three metres, if I could find a foothold, I planted a tree and—*cha-ching!*—earned myself another dime. With every heart-pounding loss of footing or sharp descent toward the bottom of the cliff, I repeated the same line from our crew's mantra in my head: *I have the choice to decide what kind of an attitude I'll have today.*

It wasn't the chill of the rain and wind, the threat of poison ivy, or the number of hours still left in the day that determined my attitude. No external factor could pronounce my day to be good or bad—not even that crushing feeling in my lungs, the weight of the planting bags chafing my shoulders, or the strain in my back and knees from climbing over logs and through slash. The power rested in my own thinking, which was my responsibility alone. Only I could decide to enjoy the day, no matter how much it snowed or hailed or how annoying the swarms of horseflies were as they buzzed around my head.

I was one of a few women who had signed up for a summer of tree planting, so I was used to belonging to an underestimated minority. Our bodies weren't built as naturally strong as the men in camp, regardless of how hard we trained at the gym in the off-season. Yet the women were usually the last ones to quit or get fired, and none of us seemed to give up. We thrived with knowing that attitude—the one factor we could control— was a key determinant of success as a planter.

The illuminating discovery that adversity held the potential to strengthen character and build endurance was what motivated me to return summer after summer. It was never about money. After all, there were easier ways to pay for post-secondary education than by living out of a tent for a summer and doing thousands of weighted squats every day in the sweltering heat.

Adversity, as I discovered, is not inherently bad. It can unleash the potential of a person's will and reveal the resilience of the human spirit. As easy as it is to resent it in the moment, it seems that it's through trials and difficult circumstances that one's true capacities can be revealed.

When Vocation Becomes Arduous

When I first started dreaming of creating radical world change at seven years old, nobody warned me of how dangerous it was to have a heart that beats for justice.

As I grew up imagining myself working to end homelessness and hunger, nobody told me my ambitions were too idealistic. When I began pursuing a post-secondary degree in justice studies, few of my professors cautioned me about the ramifications of the life of a humanitarian. Even when I started working full-time for social justice organizations, none of my superiors advised me to be wary of how easy it is to be derailed by this kind of work. Nobody told me I was entering a labyrinth of chaos and heartbreak.

I suppose there are some things in life nobody can prepare you for.

I was compelled to a vision for justice when I was about seven years old—but my dreams were in stark contrast with reality. My pursuits have not been cushioned by heartwarming accolades, sustained by sentiments of fulfillment, or inflated by easy victories. Instead, my journey has been refined by fire and sharpened by iron.

With my own eyes, I've seen how a corrupt and complacent tyrannical government can fail its suffering, starving, and subjugated people. I've seen for myself the clear-cut forests in my country and the environmental destruction committed for the sake of profit. I've seen the sallow faces and stunted bodies of gaunt, undernourished children begging for pennies in Southeast Asia and the desperate eyes of migrant workers labouring in the strawberry fields of Latin America. I've looked into the lustful eyes of men who prowl the streets of the red light district in Amsterdam to purchase access to women's bodies, as if they were a commodity. And I've seen the faces of some of those women, their expressions looking as if they were somewhere between still searching for a way out and losing all hope for a different life.

My path has been littered by disappointment, hijacked by discouragement, and challenged by adversity. And to be honest, I can't say that I'm grateful for the trials themselves. They hurt too much in the moment and haunt me too much in the aftermath. But I'm grateful for what came from them. Because it's these same things that created a space for resilience and beauty to grow.

Vocational adversity is distressing and may even be destructive, but it can also refine. With each hardship comes an opportunity to convert it into a productive enterprise. I believe every trial I've had—whether or not I'd want to relive it again—has fortified my endurance to seek justice.

Sometimes, the outcomes of my ambitions have left me wounded. Other times, they've manifested as a callous: a mark of the stress the trial caused me. A faded insignia to remind me of the toughened skin it gave me.

Finding a Place for Idealism in a Realist's World

My dreams of seeking justice have led me to some of the ugliest places and through the darkest times. The same vision I fantasized about as a seven-year-old left me as a disappointed, discouraged, disillusioned twentysomething. So how do the ambitions of a broken-hearted dreamer fit into this messy, chaotic battlefield? Is there still a place for idealism in a realist's world?

I wondered these same things as an impressionable liberal arts student, when business students and majors in medicine often told me that I'd never be able to find a "real" job. People often suggested I pursue a more practical route than studying justice. Something less idealistic. Because these days, idealism is unpopular. It's seen as a defective and invalid belief system. Might as well aspire to be a prima ballerina or a UFC champion or to live in another galaxy.

Nothing is more frustrating than feeling I have to validate my work. Often I've been accused of romanticizing my role as a humanitarian, even challenged and told, "You'll never be able to end child labour or human trafficking." And I'd never dispute that. I know I can't singlehandedly free the two hundred thousand children enslaved throughout the world and put them all into schools that I personally help build, brick by brick. Being an idealist doesn't make me naive.

I know I can't accomplish the eradication of forced child labour on my own. But I *can* be a part of projects that are protecting children from violence and preventing child trafficking from happening in the first place. I can teach families about child rights, help improve access to decent schools, and work to create better economic opportunities for parents to be able to send their kids to school.

I can't do everything, especially not on my own. But I can do something. That's all any of us can do.

Redeeming Our Trials

During a sabbatical one fall, I met up with my friend Keturah in New York City for a therapeutic weekend of sharing about our work in social justice advocacy. Crunching autumn leaves under our feet as we meandered through Central Park, I told her how I occasionally struggled with feeling as if my idealism made me weak. I lamented that I'd been born in the wrong generation—that I would've fit in so much better during the early women's suffrage era or the peaceful protests during the hippie movement in the 1960s—or any other moment in history that would appreciate and embrace the dreamer in me.

I'll never forget her response. Looking me straight in the eyes, she said, "Or maybe you're meant to be who you are now, in *this* place, in *this* generation."

And that's why still I call myself an idealist: because this generation needs people who still believe it's worthwhile to serve the oppressed. People who still believe in re-planting those empty blocks of treeless land. People who think it's worth their time to give love and foster hope for those born into a life of struggling. To advocate for the freedom of people who have had no say or have no other option.

Naturally, as a bona fide idealist learning to become more balanced as a humanitarian, I've needed to adjust my expectations of myself and of justice. Because as I found out, a tender heart gets beaten up. It brings you to your knees upon finding out that one of your students with special needs has disappeared. It tears you apart every time you read the news in the Middle East or watch a documentary about the plight of refugees. Sometimes a tender heart stops being able to feel at all.

As I discovered, one of the hardest parts of having a tender heart is that it's nearly impossible to work through humanitarian crises without crisis coming into your own life. And when it happens, not everything can happen at once. You can't go through the worst kind of brokenness and expect every piece to heal immediately. When a tender heart is cracked and crushed, it takes a long time to repair it.

Some pieces will take longer to mend than others. Others will forever be cracked and jagged. But piece by piece, when the healing comes, it comes with greater reinforcement—a new kind of strength. Scars start to scab, building resilience, enhancing character.

We all need some level of adversity to push us out of our comfort zones, to grow in unexpected ways, to learn lessons we'd never otherwise encounter. We need to be pushed—just not pushed so hard that we burn out in the process.

The magical potential about tender hearts is when their hopeful outlook is paired with realistic goals. We tender-hearted idealists don't always assume we have the power to solely eradicate complex injustices that are deeply systemic and imbued with crime, corruption, and coercion. We've seen how bad things can get, but we also know how good things can get too.

We're not blind to the obstacles. We're simply unwilling to let them be a deterrent.

CHAPTER 17

A Season for Everything: Seeking Balance in the Beauty and Burdens

There is a time for everything, and a season
for every purpose under Heaven.
A time to be born and a time to die; a time
to plant and a time to uproot.
A time to kill and a time to heal; a time
to tear town and a time to build.
A time to weep and a time to life; a time
to mourn and a time to dance.
—Ecclesiastes 3:2–4 NIV

Sheets of thunderous rain poured from an unrelenting sky, blocking my vision as I wrestled to steer my motorbike into the garage. Drenched from the humid rain, my clothes clung to my body as if I had jumped into a lake fully clothed. I kicked off my flip-flops—too slippery to wear—and carried them in one hand with a bag of mangos and papayas in the other. Barefoot and carefree, I splashed my way through the flooded street back to my house.

I wasn't irritated that my trip to the market had been rained out. I'd been expecting it. It was monsoon season in Southeast Asia, after all, which meant that every day, the sky would become clouded over by mid-afternoon and release heavy sheets of rain for a few hours from June until November.

Locals were wiser than I, so they knew to arrange their activities around the anticipated daily downpour. Every year, they prepare themselves for monsoon season with the same rituals, just as my fellow Canadians back at home would prepare themselves for winter by bringing snowsuits and studded winter tires out of hibernation. Here, Cambodians carry garbage bags on themselves at all times to use as makeshift ponchos, and they never, ever use carpets. They know that leaving their house at any given time is a risk, because the torrential downpours might leave them stranded for hours at a time. They even build their houses on stilts to protect themselves from the floodwaters.

When I think back to the rain in Cambodia, I recall what a full-body experience it was. I can hear it, feel it, taste it, smell it. I remember how deafeningly loud it was while hammering against the tin roof of my house, how I'd have to yell over the thundering reverberations in order to carry a conversation with someone. My back porch would turn into a culvert as the waters rose, creating a gentle current of beer cans and other debris that floated downstream from my neighbour's house.

Fields of rice would become lakes. Children would bathe and splash around in ditches brimming with murky water. Motorbikes would slow to a standstill as tires churned thick layers of mud, which swallowed up flip-flops and other footwear from those who had to get off to push.

Twice a year, the direction of the Tonlé Sap river changes. During the first part of the year, it drains into the Mekong river flowing down from Vietnam. In August, the Mekong starts to swell from the heavy rains and melted water from the Himalayas. Its volume surge reverses the flow back up the Tonlé Sap, often causing substantial flooding.

When a local first told me about this phenomenon, I was confused by how animated and even pleased his voice sounded as he spoke about the flooding. Hailing from a Western nation, I've always associated flooding with destruction—even death. Where I came from, flooding meant damaged homes and broken lives.

Yet in Cambodia, where the country's dark history still permeates modern life, people don't always perceive the flooding to be inherently bad. Locals have learned to use it to their advantage. Every year, thousands of people depend on that flooding, as it creates a natural hatchery for fishers. In fact, some people's livelihoods rely almost entirely on this flooding, either on a subsistence level to feed their families or as a business venture by selling and trading the fish for profit.

Within the same thing that causes damage also contains the potential for prosperity.

Destroying and Refining

Sometimes, adverse circumstances can serve you for the better. Sometimes, even the rainy seasons of your life can bring fruitfulness.

When I was nineteen, I started developing a sense of appreciation for life's rainy seasons during my first summer as a tree planter. I spent three months living out of a tent and earned ten cents for each tree I planted, but it roughened and toughened me up like no other experience I'd had. That summer, I learned not only how to conquer adversity but also how to use adversity to serve me for the better.

With the revelatory discovery of adversity's refining power at the forefront, I came home from each summer of tree planting a little bit stronger, a little more confident, a little more assured that I could tackle any obstacle. At first, I applied the endurance I built from tree-planting boot camp to my regimented study habits. When I pushed myself in university the same way I pushed myself to plant trees, I found out I could write four papers in under twenty-four hours without breaks or complaint and still earn an A. It wasn't easy, but the key is that it was possible.

And so I decided to take my ethos of endurance to other aspects of my life. In my travels and international work placements, I harnessed my mental training to overcome every challenge of foreign living. I endured the nine-hour bus rides crowded with noisy people and squawking chickens without flinching. I walked through smelly markets lined with heckling vendors, sneaky pickpocketers, and butchered animal carcasses without fear or disgust. I told myself it could always be worse.

Somehow, I'd even found it appropriate to administer this way of thinking in relationships, believing I could persevere through any interpersonal clash, no matter how ugly. I ended up staying in relationships longer than I should have—not because I wanted to stay, but because I knew I could handle their ugliness.

Adversity, to me, was a form of tough love. Its presence existed to improve and enrich me. It didn't occur to me until it was too late that my glorification of adversity could also get me into trouble.

Once I'd departed from my summers spent tree planting and eventually wound up fighting human trafficking in Cambodia, adversity took on an entirely new form. Considering mosquitoes to be a nuisance or a minor obstacle while I planted to trees transitioned into living in a country where mosquitoes carried diseases that could send me to the hospital or even kill me. Carrying heavy bags of trees all day metamorphosed into carrying the burdens of the people I served who lived under a despotic political regime, the oppression of poverty, and the cruelty of exploitation.

This was no ordinary kind of adversity. This wasn't simply a routine test of my limits in a different context, in a different vocation, in a different lifestyle. This was the kind of adversity that broke me to pieces.

Even before factoring in the traumatizing content of my anti-trafficking work, the accumulative effect of being a Westerner living in rural Cambodia was exhausting enough. I lived in a cockroach-infested house and developed a routine of toting around a broom and bug spray at all times, killing upwards of thirty creepy, crawly cockroaches per day. In addition to attempted break-ins by humans, my house also attracted unwanted guests of the rat, venomous spider, and malaria-carrying mosquito variety.

It was a year of close calls, compromised sleep, and precarious living. On one occasion, my low-quality fire hazard of an oven exploded while I was cooking, shattering my hearing for a split second and engulfing my entire kitchen in smoke and ashes. I seemed to draw in disasters because on multiple other occasions, I was electrocuted, burned by the exhaust pipe of a motorbike, and nearly involved in a crash while riding on the back of a taxi motorbike driven by a beer-guzzling driver. I was detained, threatened, and unjustly fined at the Thai-Cambodian border while attempting to get home after a series of riots, bombings, and political tensions in the nation's capital had warranted my evacuation.

Beyond the physical safety issues and discomforts, I faced a new kind of adversity. Some would call it spiritual warfare. Some might call it depression, post-traumatic stress, or burnout—perhaps even a mix of all the above. Others might say it's the harsh inevitability of a hard-working perfectionist doing humanitarian work overseas. No matter how a person branded it, what I saw and felt and experienced was much more than an enjoyable challenge or a productive trial.

Life in rural Cambodia was arduous enough on its own. But with my frame of reference as a tree planter, knowing I could persevere through even the most-treacherous circumstances, I thought I had to make my life in Cambodia even harder. When I had the opportunity to leave, I refused to take it. When support came my way, I denied it.

What I didn't realize was that just because I *could* push myself didn't mean I *should*.

Measuring Our Worthiness

Adversity is almost a form of currency in the social justice sphere. Humanitarians sometimes try to compare scars, evaluating who's been through the worst of the worst. If you haven't witnessed a traumatic event, if you haven't been part of a relief effort for a major natural disaster, if you haven't suffered from at least one tropical illness, then you haven't endured enough chaos to qualify as a real humanitarian. The harder you've had it, the better it is. The worse it's been, the stronger you are.

We seek the most difficult route possible because we think it's a greater measure of our worthiness. We forget about the strength that rests in our vulnerability or the beauty that's found in rest.

For me, being broken by trials meant two things. First, it refined my character by fire, making me stronger out of my weakness. But eventually, my strength made me weaker. It showed me that my relationship with adversity can be taken too far. Whenever I allowed trials to drive and consume my life, whenever I sought out the most-challenging opportunities to affirm my worthiness—that was when adversity stopped serving me and started harming me.

Perhaps the point isn't to seek out suffering but to find ways to redeem the suffering that will inevitably invade all our lives. Or to allow ourselves the gift of taking a break, even in the midst of chaos. Or to be content in times of stillness, knowing that we have nothing to prove.

The question is not whether or not we will face adversity. It *will* find us—in some form, at some time, to some degree. The question lies in how we choose to respond to adversity. Owning your feelings in an adverse situation doesn't mean being isolated from emotion. Choosing your thoughts about a difficult circumstance doesn't mean having to choose ironclad tenacity every single time. Controlling your reactions doesn't mean morphing into a robot or numbing away the pain.

It isn't about defeating adversity to prove ourselves but about allowing it to reveal the deepest parts of ourselves. It's not about comparing or competing for greater battle wounds, because everyone's struggle is valid. Everyone's pain is relative to his or her own experience and context. It's not about actively seeking out the hardest route possible but about embracing the course we find ourselves on now.

Finding the Balance

We need humanitarians who are hard workers. But we also need them to strive for balance. We need humanitarians who can harmonize work with rest, perseverance with self-care, pain with peace.

None of us are perfect, so none of us are ever fully balanced. There's no magic formula to master the tension between disengagement and overworking, between asceticism and excess. As one of my mentors, Kevin, once told me, "The goal is not of balance, but of balancing. We need to minimize the swing."

As a foreman of a tree-planting crew, I quickly had to learn this art of balancing—especially when it came to driving a truck in the backcountry. Even though I grew up in a small farming community in the Prairies, where my playground had been fields of hay bales and the barns of dairy cows, I had never learned how to drive a pickup. My most distressing fear that summer wasn't the responsibility of protecting my crew from grizzly bears and wild cougars—it was having to manoeuvre a hefty, oversized Ford F-350 with six hefty, oversized tree planters and thousands of trees down the precarious logging roads of northwestern British Columbia.

My best friend, Sarah—and my only other female foreman cohort that summer—knew I was intimidated by my driving responsibilities, so she took it upon herself to tutor me. A few days before our planters arrived to our planting camp for the summer, Sarah drove us to a logged block of land in the middle of nowhere and told me to get out and back up the truck.

"Back it up where?" I asked quizzically. She had parked on a curving slope without even so much as a rudimentary pullout or patch of gravel to back into.

"Up the hill," she told me in a calm but commanding voice.

"You want me to back this truck all the way up this huge, winding hill?" I asked in disbelief. In my defense, the Ford F-350 truck was gargantuan. Not only that, but it had a canopy mounted in the bed of the truck, making it awkwardly top-heavy and restricting visibility, since the canopy blocked the rear-view mirror. Everything behind me was a blind spot, aside from the little I could see from my side mirrors—which proved to be an even greater challenge to use in reverse.

"Yeah, it's good practice backing a truck up a hill. You'll spend half your day as a foreman driving backwards over all kinds of terrain," Sarah said, smiling as she added, "and don't worry, I'll teach you how to winch yourself out of a mud hole next."

Reluctantly, I shifted into reverse and started backing up— straight into a bush that separated us from a slight cliff. Sarah yelled something about how I can't drive like that unless I want to kill off my crew, so I sighed and tried again. This time, I swerved into a bush on the other side of the road, which separated us from a slight mountain.

It took us about twenty minutes to get to the top of the hill in reverse. I spent most of that time dancing the truck from side to side, nearly crashing into solid rock on the one side or nearly careening off the cliff on the other side. During this entire escapade, Sarah sat supportively in the passenger's seat, encouraging me to keep a steady rhythm instead of cranking the wheel too far to one side or the other.

By the end of the summer, I wasn't ready to enter any driving obstacle courses, but at least I was more comfortable with driving in reverse. I'd discovered how counterproductive it was to swing recklessly from one side to the other. I walked away from that summer with a valuable new skill: learning to steer by making small adjustments. Learning to work by balancing.

To be honest, I've never been particularly skilful with maintaining equilibrium outside of driving trucks either. Many different areas of my life are way off balance because I swing from one extreme to the other. As a university student, I tended to fall to the far side of the continuum by camping out at the library for the majority of my student career to study compulsively.

I would bring three meals in Tupperware containers with me to the library so I wouldn't have to abandon my studies for even a second. Because I went to extreme lengths to be the best student I could be, the girls in my dormitory went to equally extreme lengths to force me into taking a break—even removing the hinges from my bedroom door and kidnapping me to take me off campus for fresh air and perspective.

One of my few non-academic activities as a student was practicing yoga. What yoga taught me was something I needed to apply to all aspects of my life: how to slightly modify my position to keep a posture of stability. Not for a moment would I be completely uniform, so it involved a process of constantly realigning myself to avoid flailing my limbs and hopping wildly from side to side.

When I started applying my technique in yoga to my studies, the rest of my university career took a very different course. I started making small changes to my schedule, adding in weekend camping trips and coffee dates with friends, which always helped me return to my scholarly duties feeling more refreshed and productive. No, I was never fully balanced. Some outings with friends went a little too long and meant I had to compensate with an obscenely late night of writing papers. Other times, I went overboard with studying and had to take a full weekend off in order to recalibrate. It was an ongoing process of adjustment, just like correcting myself from over-steering a truck.

Absolute equilibrium is impossible to attain. Whether as a friend or daughter, traveller or employee, it seems to me that my life is instead a succession of re-balancing. And in my experience, in no other place is it more imperative that I strive to maintain a steady pace than in my work as a justice advocate. Some days, I swerve to one extreme: plunging into an impassioned rampage of mercy, pouring my entire mind, body, and soul into my work. But when that becomes fatiguing and unsustainable, I end up overcompensating by swerving to the other extreme of helpless exhaustion and even indifference.

Cranking myself way off to one side or the other—from overextending myself in seeking justice to feeling apathetic to it—is one of the worst things I can do. If I don't give enough of myself, I am not fulfilling my potential or my values of integrity, service, and honour. If I give too much of myself, I become unhealthy and isolated, bitter and resentful.

As a fallible human, I can't expect to dwell in a homeostatic bliss. But I *can* aim for a more sustainable way of living. It's okay to have ambitious goals, like ameliorating injustice, but it's also okay to hold on to my freedom and enjoy my blessings as I use them for the benefit of others. I won't always get it right, but at minimum, I can try. Because learning to strike the balance between any two extremes is more of a journey than a destination.

Coming to Grips with the Grips of Adversity

As the floodwaters in Cambodia rise during the monsoon season, they create a means for fishers to better support their livelihoods in a beautifully redemptive way. But if the waters rise too much, they end up desecrating fields and houses and livelihoods. The same thing that creates fruitfulness can also cause destruction and chaos.

During my time in Cambodia, I saw a lot of rain—in the literal and metaphorical sense. Without it, I wouldn't grow. With too much of it, I would drown.

Just like the monsoons in Southeast Asia, adversity comes with both prosperous and destructive potential. Sometimes we need injustice and seasons of rain to break us before we can respond to others in a meaningful, effective form of solidarity, where we can sincerely say, "I've been there too." Adversity can serve us—but only when balanced by thriving in other aspects of life. Too much adversity—or perhaps *how* adversity is sought—can be damaging.

Pursuing justice is bound to come with an inextricable tangle of adverse ramifications. It's the kind of work that has the inherent potential to deflate one's energy, diminish one's spirit, even break one's heart. But after my work in Southeast Asia as a justice advocate, experiencing monsoon season reminded me of the need to find my own equilibrium. To live as Charles Dudley Warner once phrased it: to make "the journey of this life with just baggage enough." To find ways to live well and beautifully and justly, all at the same time. To seek that balance between rain and sun, between experiencing grace and truth, between holding on and letting go.

Because for everything, there is a season.

CHAPTER 18

Flourishing in Community: Finding My Way Home

Two are better than one, because they
have a good return for their labour:
If either of them falls down, one can help the other up.
Though one may be overpowered,
two can defend themselves.
A cord of three strands is not quickly broken.
—Ecclesiastes 4:9-10, 12 NIV

Through bleary eyes, I watched the beaten-up blue Tempo roll out of the parking lot and point southward. As two sets of hands waved their bittersweet goodbye from rolled-down windows, there was only word on my mind: *community*.

I needed community.

Standing at a crossroads—both literally and metaphorically—I could feel my heart being pulled in a million contrasting directions. Part of me stubbornly wanted to continue pursuing the venturesome life of a humanitarian expatriate. For years, all I'd known was working deep in the trenches of human trafficking prevention across international borders. But as I watched my friends become engulfed by traffic and disappear into a blazing California sunrise, the other part of me couldn't remember why I had uprooted myself to begin with.

For the first time, this nomadic lifestyle of mine—and its series of six-month job contracts and non-permanent living situations, its temporary friendships and endless stream of goodbyes—it all seemed more exhausting than appealing.

I found myself mechanically walking by instinct down the street to an orange brick café tucked away in a corner of Little Italy. During my short-term stay in San Diego, the café had compelled me daily into its inviting quarters. Every time, the same barista would greet me warmly in Italian and ask if I wanted one or two additional shots of espresso—as if it was non-optional to consume caffeine in regular quantities. But no matter how strong and robust the coffee was, how beautiful the rise and fall of the Italian opera playing softly in the background, or how much the atmosphere of the café took me back to my travels in Italy, it wasn't the espresso that kept drawing me back in.

Even before I'd stepped both feet into the café, I heard the singsongy voice of the same brown-eyed, bubbly barista— her voice punctuated by a rich Italian accent—hollering, "*Buongiorno*, Katie!"

She knew my name.

Freedom in Fellowship

After seven years, the draining nature of my vagabond lifestyle and the anonymity of my travels had finally caught up with me. I was as desperate for consistent human connection as the city of San Diego was desperate for rain in its drought. Both the city and I were in want of something we did not have. Both of us had run dry and were in dire need of nourishment.

As grinding espresso machines and Pavarotti's operatic tenor competed for attention in the background of the café, I wondered at what point I had begun operating in survival mode rather than living joyously. Hopping from country to country, from one humanitarian crisis to the next, had originally seemed to be the perfect blend of adventure and altruism. Wasn't this the life I'd always wanted?

What can start out as valiant acts of selflessness so often turn into obstinate acts of self-indulgence. Over time, the most influential forces in my life—from my supervisors to my faith background, from my social justice training to my own stubborn unwillingness to be vulnerable—had glorified the ethos of doing life alone. My need for a ferocious brand of independence had gradually spread like poison through my veins, convincing me that I couldn't live a life of meaning in comfort, only in chaos. Living beautifully was no longer an option.

Going home wasn't possible anymore either. In my circle of justice workers, there is an assumption that humanitarians only live overseas in developing countries. We bypass the problems and the need to help communities in Western nations because we believe living a comfortable life is morally inferior to roughing it overseas.

I too bought into the belief that my home in Canada wasn't conducive to the calibre of challenge I wanted. Life seemed too easy. And that was how I wound up living in one of the seediest towns in Cambodia, riddled with casinos and brothels, where some of the darkest things in the world happen in plain daylight. It seemed to be the kind of conditions where I could be sufficiently challenged. Because, to me, the tougher route was always better. And the tougher route always meant the solo route.

Sipping a cappuccino in solitude, as hazy streams of California sunshine filtered through the window of that Italian coffee shop, a series of fragmented memories of seasons I'd spent alone began haunting me all at once—seasons where I leaned into uncompromising solitude rather than in the sanctuary of community: That summer I'd lived in a cabin nearly in total seclusion, those two months I'd backpacked solo through Eastern Europe, the arduous days I'd spent tree planting alone while completely sequestered from human contact. I thought back to that empty, cockroach-infested house I'd lived in all by myself in Cambodia, with no Internet access and little contact with my friends and family back at home.

Such austere and isolated conditions had surely served a purpose. The adversity and seclusion had created a platform for my character to be refined, my mind to be challenged, and my soul to learn how to persevere in spite of physical injury, emotional distress, and spiritual chaos.

But those harsh eras of solitude had not been moments of flourishing.

My embittering habit of prioritizing the cause of my work ahead of my relationships and my own basic human needs had left me so depleted, so wilted. I was tired of farewells, tired of the ache of anonymity, tired of the weariness from wandering … So tired that the sight of hands waving goodbye from an old blue Tempo or a familiar face greeting me by name in an urban café was enough to break me down into pieces.

The more I pondered, the more I realized my moments of wholehearted flourishing were always experienced in community. Not the kind of community encountered passively, by default, or on social media, but real, authentic, and deliberate face-to-face community. The kind of community that looks like grace, feels like love, and manifests itself as peace.

Community was she and I sharing the secrets of our kindred souls while collecting sea glass along an abandoned white-sand beach. It was the moment of bonding when he and I realized we shared more common gifts and burdens than we'd ever imagined at first glance.

It was the endless stream of laughter and tears as my best friend and I camped our way through Canada and the wordless exchange of smiles as my sister and I stood in the middle of the silent snow-capped Alps—the place we'd been compelled to visit ever since we first watched *The Sound of Music* together as children.

Community was found in the small comfort of sharing a single tea bag with a close friend while living far from home in a foreign country—the last tea bag I'd salvaged from my stash of Canadian delicacies. It was the childlike wonder and whimsy that came from flying over stunning mountaintop vistas in a helicopter with a treasured travel partner, or the simple joy of watching sunset skies sinking into a still ocean on a camping trip with old friends.

Every communal meal, every porch-swing conversation, every summer evening of strumming guitars while encircling campfires with friends who made imprints on my heart—these were the moments I came alive. These were the moments where hurt could be converted into healing, loneliness replaced by communion, and disappointment transformed into hope.

That was the realization that hit me in that California coffee shop: It was possible to survive in isolation, but it was in community that I could thrive.

When I left San Diego, I returned to my home in Canada with a new plan. It wasn't to push harder, move faster, or work longer. It was to love fearlessly, speak honestly, and bond more with others. It was to candidly ask for help and be receptive to other people's care. It was to live out Caedmon's call to forge connections with each person in our lives with the sincere intention to "cradle a sense of wonder in their life, to honour the hard-earned wisdom of their sufferings, to waken their joy … [and say] 'I know—I understand.'"

Yes, adamantly abiding by absolute self-sufficiency helped to give me greater tenacity. Yes, it takes a great amount of strength to live a life of resolute independence. But it takes courage to live in community. And from this courage comes an outcome of the purest and most wholehearted kind: life lived abundantly.

Creating Community

I've travelled to many places of the world, always wondering when community would finally find me. I'm now realizing community is up to me to create.

The thing about community is that it's easier to find while living and traveling abroad because everyone else is equally prepared to be vulnerable in meeting other people. Backpackers and expats are like a bunch of kindergarteners on their first day of school, shamelessly approaching their peers to ask, "Will you be my friend? Will you come climb with me to this castle or join me on this boat tour or find a cozy café we can warm up in and have a cappuccino together?"

While backpacking in Montenegro, I was thumbing through a travel book for my next destination, Serbia, from the corner of an old Romanesque youth hostel when a bubbly Australian girl approached me and asked, "Hey, do you want to come on a road trip with us? We need one more person to fill up our rental car."

I shrugged my shoulders and casually replied, "Yeah, maybe. Where are you going?"

"We're not too sure, but I just met a couple of other backpackers who are thinking of doing a two-day loop around the country to check out the mountains up north and doing some hiking. We're going to leave tomorrow morning before sunrise. You in?"

"Oh, sure. Sounds fun." I closed my book and joined the planning committee, comprised of the Australian woman, an American Peace Corps volunteer, and a young gentleman from

Spain who was taking a year away from school to travel. With little more than an exchange of first names, the four of us sat around a wooden table lit by dripping Gothic candles, spread a weathered map of Montenegro before us, and started planning our trip together.

That was that. I had made three new friends and lined up a new adventure to add to my itinerary in the blink of an eye.

When I started my reintegration back home in Canada, the process of attaching myself to a community looked much different. Part of it was because I was lagging far behind everybody in a cultural sense. After all, I'd left North America right before it had seemed to become mandatory for everyone to have an iPhone and a Pinterest account. So when I came back, I did not know what the fox said or what kind of style Gangnam might be. I had never heard of Candy Crush, Songza, or a "selfie" before. I'd missed the pregnancy and birth of Prince William and Kate's first child and I didn't know that Margaret Thatcher had passed away that year. I'd felt like a foreign exchange student in my own country—but the kind of foreign exchange student who had been living under a rock for quite some time.

Being so far out of the loop meant I had to live on the fringes for a while. I had forgotten how difficult it was to find community— especially in a context where a career, marital status, or wedding invitations mattered more than the next country you were travelling to or what personal epiphany you made that day while hiking along a fjord. Back at home, your job—not your travel ambitions, your dreams, or even your personality— defined your identity. Making friends in this context was not nearly as simple as approaching a random traveller in a youth hostel to say, "Hi there, let's be friends. Come with me and a bunch of other strangers on a road trip and we'll get to know each other as we travel together."

There's something about community that's so hard and rare to find, yet it's the one thing we can't live without.

The Power of Partnerships

My hair stylist, Franco*, is a Filipino man who moved to Canada shortly after Typhoon Haiyan hit the Philippines on November 8, 2013. When I first met Franco, he told me about his arduous journey from Manila to Winnipeg, a decision he made for the express purpose of making a better income to support his wife and children back home. He also told me about the chaos and destruction he witnessed as the typhoon, which claimed 10,000 lives and left twelve million people at risk and stranded for help, ripped through his country.

Had I not recently returned from my service in Cambodia at the time that the typhoon struck, I likely would've been deployed to assist in the relief efforts. Instead, like much of the rest of the world, I watched the devastating footage of the typhoon from TV screens, read the newspaper headlines, and received the urgent emails from aid agencies making appeals for donations. I kept up-to-date through Facebook updates and emails from friends who had been sent to different parts of the Philippines to partake in relief efforts. No matter how informed I tried to be, I couldn't imagine what people like Franco and his family

---

*   Note: Name has been changed.

had been through during the storm and in the cataclysmic aftermath.

Franco had given me a gut-wrenchingly honest report of what it was like to have lived through Typhoon Haiyan. It was a lot of heavy information for me to take in, but the one hopeful thing I gleaned from his story was when he'd said, "The amazing thing about the typhoon was seeing the response from the international community. They're the ones who helped us the most."

That's the power of partnership. That's the strength that comes from collaboration.

From the individual news reports of the typhoon, there was an underlying sense of overwhelming grief and desperation. But from the intricate web of efforts combined came forward movement. From the assemblage of agencies who used their own instruments of justice blended together in harmonious concert, there was a sense of greater hope.

Once the worst surges of the typhoon had quelled, NGOs poured into the Philippines to work together in their emergency relief efforts. While some NGOs focused on providing mosquito nets, blankets, food rations, candles, protective tarps, and hygiene items, other organizations addressed the loss of livelihood, security, and dignity faced by survivors. Each NGO was an indispensable spoke of a wheel that moved the country toward a state of long-term holistic recovery. Each one drew upon its own strengths as an invaluable piece of the puzzle.

UNICEF and Save the Children had strived to meet the physical and educational needs of the four million Filipino children who were affected by the storm. Agencies like Oxfam and Hope for the Sold honed in on the fact that natural disasters create fertile breeding grounds for traffickers who prey on people in vulnerable situations. They came to the aid of the three million displaced persons and placed a special emphasis on the women and orphaned children who were at higher risk for violence, abuse, and exploitation.

Several NGOs employed a divide-and-conquer method by flocking to as many different regions of the country as possible. Habitat for Humanity assessed damages on the central islands and began constructing new houses, while the organization I'd worked for in Cambodia reached out to some of the oft-forgotten remote islands, where mothers and children stood in debris holding heart-stopping signs that read, "Need help: we are hungry and thirsty".

Other agencies viewed the typhoon through a lens of long-term recovery and development. CARE had called for aid supplies to be sourced from local markets. Many NGOs hired Filipino staff to carry out relief efforts to stimulate local employment. World Relief developed strong partnerships with local relief agencies, churches, and governmental partners to reconstruct shelters and churches and to provide social services to families.

No country will ever be the same after a natural disaster or a civil war, but the best way to contribute to the restoration process is when communities from near and far come together in solidarity as a global family, protecting and loving the brothers and sisters they have never met.

The Gift of Community

Community is constructed on a foundation of partnerships. Whether it's between two people or a conglomerate of agencies, a partnership is what gives breath and a heartbeat to any functioning system—be it a family or a church, a non-profit or a corporation.

A partnership is not a business transaction. It's not a distant or indifferent interaction between closed-off parties. A partnership is a partnership when both sides are willing to let the walls come down. It's only as effective as the level of authenticity and trust the partnership has as it moves along its trajectory.

On the most practical, relational, and intimate level, one of the greatest places I've learned about partnership is along the messy yet beautiful journey I've had with my boyfriend. We're partners. And that means he loves and supports me no matter how hard it is sometimes. He sticks by me even when I'm a ball of stress or an emotional wreck, like that day not too long ago when he had accidentally broken his expensive stained-glass Montreal Canadiens lamp and *he* had to comfort *me* as I sobbed uncontrollably in a puddle of exhaustion. And I still love and support him, even when I think he's too old to wear a t-shirt with a graphic of a shark on a surfboard or when he thinks it's okay to wear plaid shorts and a plaid shirt at the same time in public.

That's the beauty about partnerships—they can remain steadfast even in the hardest and ugliest times. And that's why community is such a gift: It creates an abundance of joy and comfort, solutions and resources. It brings together a constellation of ideas and perspectives, whether or not you agree with them, and offers space for them to be spoken and practiced.

For me, the reason why it's been critically important to learn about partnership from every angle is because of its paramount role in seeking justice. It's through partnerships that we can fight egregious evils like human trafficking or restore a region after a tropical storm. It's in community that we build the momentum to become more powerful than exploitation and poverty and destruction.

The power of partnership applies to both the process and the outcome. For me, learning to do community well in a justice context is not only about having collaborative strategies to combat evil for the sake of others but also to ensure that I—as a helper—have a safety net of people I can fall back on whenever I need them. Because community is one of the things that sustains me when my hope is under siege. Community is what awakens joy, befriends justice, and threatens evil all at the same time.

And in retrospect—because the hard times always seem to make more sense in retrospect—I know I've had to go through the struggles that I did. I just didn't have to go through them alone.

CHAPTER 19

When Justice Just Is:
Hope in Wholeness

Hope is a waking dream.
—Aristotle
Hope is patience with the lamp lit.
—Tertullian
Hope is the thing with feathers
That perches in the soul,
And sings the tune without the words,
And never stops at all.
—Emily Dickinson

Seeking justice turned out to be a lot like planting trees for me.

Much like my vocation as a humanitarian, I had to come to grips with the fact that my summers of tree planting were going to be painfully difficult and that there was no way around that. Most of my days of tree planting, I worked in the middle of thick slash that scraped my body and poked me in the eye. I slipped and tripped on rocky and haphazard terrain. Often, I felt isolated and concerned about what might be lurking around the corner—a bear, perhaps, or a cougar. There was a constant threat to my safety.

The odds were almost always stacked against me. If I wasn't planting in sub-zero temperatures with snow on the ground, then I was fighting off swarms of mosquitoes and black flies in over-thirty-degree-Celsius weather. My work was tough—and most days, it seemed impossible.

After an entire day of planting, I would stand at the front of my piece of land with sweat and dirt smudging my face and look out at what seemed to be nothing. I was hardly able to see any evidence of my work. The trees were too tiny to see or were dwarfed by gnarly tree branches and piles of slash, giant fallen logs, and fields of stinging nettle and devil's club. I would go home knowing I may never see the fruits of my labour, never see the seedlings grow into towering spruces and pines.

I also couldn't protect my work. I couldn't go back and water each tree individually. I couldn't shield each one from the boiling sun, from the mountain storms or floods, or from deer and other predators. I had to accept the finite. I had to let go and reassure myself that I had done what was in my power to do. I had to walk away only with the hope that my work would be enough for my trees to become forests.

I could only do what I could, and I had to let all the rest be.

When Two Worlds Collide

In my social justice pursuits, I've journeyed across a fairly full spectrum of humanitarian endeavours. My early beginnings were with a low-funded mission plant that relied entirely on church financial offerings and could only accept staff on a volunteer basis. The organization had little credibility or recognition outside of the church, but our reputation was strong where it most mattered: among the people we worked with.

As teachers for children with special needs, we were invested not only in our students' academic lives but in their home lives as well. We were connected to our students on a deeply human level. With little or no formal training, we embarrassed ourselves and made mistakes. We developed curriculum along the way through trial and error. We acted out of visceral reactions rather than by a rule book. We were constantly in flux without adhering to a specific structure and had to do the best we could with limited resources. We weren't always as wise as we should've been, but creativity was welcomed. Freedom was encouraged. Love was the focus.

The trajectory of my humanitarian experience changed drastically as I moved on to working with a more charismatic organization after that. I entered a new world by joining a team of go-getters at a start-up non-profit in California that courted celebrities and influenced some of the most-powerful people in the country, from business executives at Google to professional athletes. I gained a one-of-a-kind experience of pursuing justice, although it was more about power than passion. And so I lost that connection between myself and the people I'd started out on this journey to serve. In this new environment, we were too busy investing in our branding and marketing to be able to invest in the communities we were trying to help.

That gap widened when I eventually moved on to work for one of the most longstanding, well-respected organizations in the relief-and-development world. We had a presence on every populated continent, but we didn't know the first names of any of the people we served. We referred to them as "beneficiaries" or "stakeholders." We called our help "interventions" or "strategies," which we developed through the lengthy administrative tasks of creating charts and logical models and fifty-page proposals.

Gone were the lengthy conversations I'd once had with co-workers about the progress or self-esteem of our struggling students or the psychological, spiritual, and relational health of their families. Now we talked about capacity building and empowerment—words we overused but didn't really understand what they meant or looked like.

Gone were the days of meeting the people I worked with on their terms, working with them to reach their own self-identified goals. Now it was a numbers game. It was more about meeting the quantitative benchmarks and outcomes within our results-based management framework that would render our projects either successful in the eyes of a funding agency or not.

Gone were the days of meaningful interactions with people in desperate times. Now our work was accomplished from a swivelling office chair in front of a computer screen instead of sitting with people in their homes. When we did have face-to-face interactions with the people we served, it was distantly through assembly lines at food distributions.

Although I resented it, I did understand the need for bureaucracy. Databases, inventory lists, monitoring and evaluation systems, and operational guidelines are a necessary part of any well-organized, functional non-profit. What didn't make sense to me, though, was spending more time on documenting our work than doing the work itself. Spending the majority of my time reporting to my supervisors and donors detracted from the time I could otherwise invest in the hearts and lives of people who needed fuller attention.

All the flip charts and strategy meetings were draining my energy, squelching my creativity, and weighing on my soul. Work relationships formed through emails and occasional Skype calls were too impersonal to be productive. Using technical terms like *beneficiaries* reduced human qualities and inherent value into a quantitative measurement of progress that was based on our own set of indicators and projected outcomes. It meant Julia, my favourite little student in Mexico, was someone I was supposed to "empower" instead of love. It meant the women I'd met who had exited sex trafficking in Athens and Amsterdam were "victims" needing to follow predetermined rehabilitation proceedings, not survivors worthy of respect and needing to be supported in an individualized way that made sense to each one of them.

At the outset of my journey, I worked in a deeply relational environment full of passion and vigour, although we were a low-capacity organization making lots of haphazard mistakes along the way. After a few years, I'd transitioned into working for a high-function, accomplished mega-organization that had a global reach but turned people into numbers and humanitarians into cogs in a machine. The former was an idealist's paradise—the latter was the quintessential niche for realists. And little did these two paradigms overlap.

There has to be a way to manage the tension between passion and rationality. Because passion isn't thoughtlessness, just as effectively designed enterprises aren't fruitless. What we need to do is limit the bureaucracy while still engaging in effective, well-researched work. We need to put the *human* back into *humanitarianism*.

What we need is for idealism and realism to coexist. And I think that camaraderie starts with hope.

Hope: A State of Mind

We've always been enchanted by the power of daring to hope for something beyond what we now know. The dreams of idealists have been forever vital in influencing the human psyche and shaping the course of history. What if Martin Luther King Jr. hadn't had a dream but had preached instead, "I have a logical five-step plan … I have a plan today!" What if John Lennon had sung, "You might say I'm pragmatic, but I'm not the only one"? What if Eleanor Roosevelt had suggested that the future belongs, in fact, to those who believe in fact and figures, rather than in "the beauty of their dreams"?

We're big on hope. And yet hope is hard. It's difficult to build and easy to destroy. It takes a long time to prevail and a short time to disappoint. It's almost impossible to grasp: it has no texture, no traction, no tangible measurement of its capacity.

Especially in my line of work with human trafficking interventions, my vocation doesn't naturally lend itself to hope. Some say as many as thirty-six million people are forced to work against their will, from inside factories to brothels, restaurants to strip clubs, in practically every country across the world—even in my own backyard in Canada.[1] How can I find hope of this kind while knowing that slavery is worse today than it ever was during the transatlantic slave trade over two hundred years ago? What is the point of hope if it's something I'm perpetually waiting for?

Within the darkness of injustice, hope can seem impossible. For those of us who spend our lives seeking justice, hope can be as rare as a meteor, as easy to work through as quantum physics, but as necessary as oxygen.

Deep down, whether we work on the field as humanitarians or in an office building of a multinational corporation, we know hope matters. Deep down, we believe in the power and significance of our dreams. Somewhere inside of us, we know seeking justice is vital, as hard and as discouraging and even hopeless as it can be. What we sometimes get wrong is what hope is really all about. We idealize it. We think of it as an emotion. We see hope as the self-pleasing desires that we plead to God to grant us.

Whenever hope means waiting for something good to happen based on our emotional impulses and whims, we're bound for disappointment. Because emotions change with circumstances. Our desires evolve over time. And so hope ultimately becomes a thing that fails to deliver. That's when hope is a hard pill to swallow.

So maybe hope isn't the problem. Maybe the problem is how we perceive it.

Romanticizing hope and thinking of it as that feeling we get when we want something to happen is the easy way out. Because, a lot of times, we hope for things to happen through a stress-free, uncomplicated, invulnerable route—one that comes without too much conflict or mistakes or regret.

I think that's why we sometimes avoid hope. It's because we're afraid. Afraid of what we could lose by taking a risk on hoping for something that might not transpire how we want. Afraid of unknown territory or an outcome we might not like. Afraid of what we might look like if we fail. We confuse hope with desire—and when the things we desire don't come to fruition exactly the way we want, then we give up. If there's even a chance that what we hope for doesn't materialize, we'd rather not try at all. "I don't want to get my hopes up," we say with a shrug, as if hope is worse than indifference.

Perhaps what we need instead is the kind of hope that's less contingent on how we feel. Because if we always let our feelings act on our behalf, we'll be held captive by them. If hope is only ever an emotion, we're less likely to do what it takes to convert it into a reality. For me, if I let the way that I feel about evil and human trafficking and exploitation to decide how I respond to it, I'll be forever immobilized.

I've learned the hard way how counterproductive it can be to have the grandiose hope for perfection. It's unrealistic to enter a service capacity with the belief that I can flawlessly remove the pain and plight of other people—or that I can even do such a thing at all. But I've also learned how futile it is to try to influence the course of justice without some level of sanguine expectations. After all, how can I help others if I don't have any hope for them to begin with?

Another problem is how often we equate hope with idealism—both of which are grossly misunderstood, especially in the humanitarian sphere. Neither hope nor idealism is naive. They're not euphemisms for ignorance or cluelessness. They're not the more colourful but less desirable alternative to realism. Not at all. Harbouring hope means having the ability to dream for the things that could actually come to life if more people were committed to dreaming about them too. Unleashing idealism is having a drive to pursue causes that the rest of the world has given up on. Both are propelled by compassionate visions, not a bottom line.

And yet hope and idealism don't need to be dichotomized with realism and then pitted against each other, either. They're all different paths to the same goal, with each path having a strength that the other does not have. After all, shameless idealists are often the instigators of creativity and innovation, the communicators of possibilities, and the constructors of alternatives. Within the mind of a hopeful idealist is the birthplace of ideas that others dare not and cannot fathom. The hopeful idealists generate and incubate the ideas for the realists to carry through with resourceful, practical, effective planning. It's not only possible for them to coexist but even for them to bolster each other and flourish.

Birds can fly, and fish can swim. But then there are loons whose haunting music echoes in the night in between bobbing and gliding underwater, and there are flying fish that propel themselves out of the water, reaching heights over four feet and distances as long as two hundred metres. There are those who retain their authenticity while borrowing from the essence of another.

Our world isn't divided strictly into dreamers and doers. Idealism and realism aren't binaries that need to be sequestered into separate categories. They exist on a continuum. There are moments when one must lean a little further one way or the other. It's the idealists who learn to appreciate the qualities of realists and the realists who reciprocate as well, who know how to effectively cooperate without losing their inner fibres.

I sincerely believe what Orison Swett Marden once said is true, that "all [people] who have achieved great things have been great dreamers."[2]

Tempered Idealism

For me, hope has become less of a feeling and has grown more into a state of mind. Hope means embracing the final outcome, no matter what it is, knowing that it will make sense. Hope is trusting in a higher power to work out everything for good, even if my expectations aren't met. Because while that "good" may not bring about the outcome I wanted, it may have a far greater purpose than what I ever imagined.

My hope comes not from an emotion, but from possessing a kind of idealism that has been tested over and over again.

It's been shaped by the extremes of love and loss while teaching kids with special needs in Latin America, whose own family members believe them to be cursed. It's been developed and stretched by seeing the remains of steel and rubble in the streets of Bosnia twenty years after the civil war. It's been intensified by witnessing the traces of carnage on the Killing Fields of Cambodia, where a malignant government continues to wreak oppression and violence on its own people. It's been sobered by seeing how a thousand years of racism has left the Romany people I've met in Hungary and Bulgaria with fewer opportunities for education, employment, health, and safety than non-Romany people. It's been fortified by meeting women exiting prostitution in my own country—some who had been trafficked, others who'd had no other option but to sell their bodies for survival.

Today, my ambitions have been tweaked, but I haven't stopped hoping or dreaming. I still call myself an idealist—but not in a blind and uncritical sense. Not with childlike oblivion. Not in the kind of way that the cynics like to criticize and belittle. Sharpened by my own experiences of disillusionment, failure, and heartbreak, I speak as someone whose idealism has been tested and challenged under the pressure of an unrelenting world that tries its best to breed doubt, delusion, and disbelief.

Now, I'd say I have a tempered idealism. Just as a piece of metal or a knife is tempered by putting it through fire to increase its durability, so has my idealism become tempered by experiencing trials and observing first-hand justice withheld. Weathered by witnessed tragedies, challenged by disappointment, and given buoyancy by setback after setback, I'd say I've earned the right to hope—the kind of hope that's based on the equally real experiences of knowing both good and bad, not as binary options but in a blended union.

And so I can plant seeds of hope in my journey of seeking justice in a similar way that I used to plant trees during my summers as a university student. I know the kind of challenges I'm up against. I know there is a high probability that not all the work I do will blossom as I want it to, if it even blossoms at all. But I know that the only way forward comes step by step, moment by moment, day by day. And even though the good may seem to be covered up by the bad for now doesn't mean it won't start to crop up later.

No, it is not a mark of naïveté to have dreams and hopes for greater things. It is neither childish nor impractical. In a world so desperately in need of those who dream with tempered idealism, it is necessary.

---

[1]   Walk Free Foundation, "The Global Slavery Index 2014," Global Slavery Index, http://www.globalslaveryindex.org/.

[2]   Orison Swett Marden, The Miracle of Right Thought (New York: Cosimo, 2007), 13.

Is Seeking Justice Worth It?

Every great dream begins with a dreamer.
Always remember, you have within you the strength,
the patience, and the passion
to reach for the stars to change the world.
—Harriet Tubman

Countless times by countless people, I've been asked the same, ubiquitous question: Is seeking justice worth it? It's an ominous question. But to be honest, it's a question I've often asked myself too.

So is it?

There's an elderly gentleman living in my neighbourhood who personifies the answer to this question. He's a man who shows me exactly what an enduring hope and commitment to justice looks like. Sometimes daily, I see this man, wearing the same blue windbreaker and black dress pants, slowly and carefully picking up trash with his bare, shaking, age-spotted hands to clear the sidewalks and back alleys of his neighbourhood.

He's not naive. He's lived long enough to know there will be more discarded pizza boxes and crumpled chip bags carelessly tossed onto the streets the next day, and the day after that. But every day, he chooses to return, tidying up the mess left by other people, leaving the path behind him a little cleaner, a little healthier, a little more beautiful.

This is a man who knows what it's like to have disappointment and ugliness littered around him—in a literal and figurative sense. Yet this is a man who chooses to not let either feelings or circumstances quash his vision for something better in his community. He knows that hope can remain even when it's submerged in darkness. He knows hope and disappointment can't be easily severed. He knows that goodness matters.

What this man shows me is that seeking justice is worth it, no matter how ugly it can get, because there is room for hope. For me, whether I'm looking into the eyes of an inner-city youth I know is being groomed by a gang for prostitution or if I'm reading yet another email about how a lack of funding is holding our non-profit back from helping the people who need it most, I must remember that hope is less of an emotion and more of a state of mind. When it comes to the fight against injustice, I cannot—will not—hush my hope.

Like seeking justice, hope is a practice. It's that thing that guides me in my pursuit for greater purposes, with the faith that whatever the outcome may be, I'll have the strength and discernment to know how to handle it.

So yes, seeking justice is worth it. It's worth it as long as justice is sought with the kind of humility that's prepared to see backsliding and failure. As long as justice makes room for the stories of journeys—sometimes with two steps forward, one step back—not just stories of success. As long as seekers of justice are prepared to see ugliness that may never go away, to meet people who may never recover, to know that not everybody is going to be saved.

Yes, of course it's worth it, although that's not really the right question. You can't divide seeking justice into the good and the bad and then try to measure one against the other. Because the weight of the bad is not equal to the value of the good.

Yes, it's worth it, because even the bad has value too. From the brokenness comes beauty. We can't diminish or undermine the impact of the bad. We can use the bad we encounter for a greater purpose—for our own redemption, for the good of others.

Yes, it's worth it, but we must seek it wisely. It is a marathon, not a sprint. It needs to be sought as if we are doctors there to pursue long-term, holistic health for our patients and not just to slap a quick fix on wounds too deep for Band-Aids. It's planting a tree one tree at a time, one hope at a time.

Yes, living justly is worth it when it's integrated with living well and beautifully at the same time, as one pursuit. It's not dehumanized humanitarianism that allows us to help others— it's having boundaries and meeting our own needs in order to thrive and inspire others to do so too. Living justly means living wholly.

My answer is yes—justice is worth it. But there's a lot more to it. With tempered idealism and a soul tethered to seeking justice, I can wage on knowing justice is not heroism or perfection, not a battle between idealism or realism. It is a seed of hope that

I plant. It is more than what I do; it is who I am. It's wholeness. It's how I live: Always within the grace and love and vulnerability of community and always worthwhile.

Why? Because justice just is.

BIBLIOGRAPHY

Amsterdam Herald. "Record Number of Tourists in Netherlands in 2011." February 2, 2012. http://amsterdamherald.com/index.php/allnews-list/124-20120202-tourism.

Andriotis, Annamaria. "10 Things the Beauty Industry Won't Tell You." *Market Watch.* April 20, 2011. http://www.marketwatch.com/story/10-things-the-beauty-industry-wont-tell-you-1303249279432.

Bornstein, David. *How to Change the World: Social Entrepreneurs and the Power of New Ideas.* New York: Oxford University Press, 2007.

Brussa, Licia, ed. *Sex Work in Europe.* Amsterdam: TAMPEP International Foundation, 2009.

Central Intelligence Agency. *The CIA World Factbook 2010.* New York: Skyhorse Publishing, 2009.

Fogel, Daniel Mark. "Upton Sinclair." *The American Novel.* March 2007. http://www.pbs.org/wnet/americannovel/timeline/sinclair.html.

Engineers Without Borders. "Failure Reports." 2011. (Accessed December 12, 2013).
http://legacy.ewb.ca/en/whoweare/accountable/failure.html.

European Roma Rights Centre. *Breaking the Silence: A Report by the European Roma Rights Centre and People in Need.* Budapest: European Roma Rights Centre and People in Need, 2011.

Goldenberg, Suzanne. "It Was like They'd Never Seen a Woman Before." *Guardian*, February 3, 2006. http://www.theguardian.com/film/2006/feb/03/gender.world.

Hunt, Katie. "Cambodia Shuts Australian-Run Orphanage over Abuse Allegations." CNN. March 26, 2013. http://www.cnn.com/2013/03/26/world/asia/cambodia-orphanage/.

Lee, Veronica. "Britain's Child Migrants." *Guardian*, April 2, 2011. http://www.theguardian.com/lifeandstyle/2011/apr/02/britain-child-migrants-australia-commonwealth.

Lupton, Robert D. *Toxic Charity: How the Church Hurts Those They Help and How to Reverse It.* New York: HarperCollins, 2011.

Marden, Orison Swett. *The Miracle of Right Thought.* New York: Cosimo, 2007.

Marks, Simon. "Somaly Mam: The Holy Saint (and Sinner) of Sex Trafficking." *Newsweek*, May 21, 2014. http://www.newsweek.com/2014/05/30/somaly-mam-holy-saint-and-sinner-sex-trafficking-251642.html.

McEchran, Rich. "Aid Workers and Post-traumatic Stress Disorder." *Guardian*, March 3, 2014. http://www.theguardian.com/global-development-professionals-network/2014/mar/03/post-traumantic-stress-disorder-aid-workers.

Obama, Barack. "Remarks by the President in the State of the Union Address." White House. January 24, 2012. http://www.whitehouse.gov/the-press-office/2012/01/24/ remarks-president-state-union-address.

Palamarchuk, Andrew. "Toronto Police's Project Spade Results in International Porn Arrests." *Inside Toronto*, March 3, 2014. http://www.insidetoronto.com/news-story/4219011-toronto-police-s-project-spade-results-in-international-child-porn-arrests/.

Perry, Suzanne. "The Stubborn 2% Giving Rate." *The Chronicle of Philanthropy.* June 17, 2013. http://philanthropy.com/article/The-Stubborn-2-Giving-Rate/139811/.

Roeger, Katie L., Amy Blackwood, and Sarah L. Pettijohn. "The Nonprofit Sector in Brief: Public Charities, Giving, and Volunteering." Urban Institute. November 1, 2011. http://www.urban.org/uploadedpdf/412434-nonprofitalmanacbrief2011.pdf.

Romero, Simon. "Quinoa's Global Success Creates Quandary at Home." *New York Times*, March 19, 2011. http://www.nytimes.com/2011/03/20/world/americas/20bolivia.html?_r=1&.

Thomas, Derek. "These 4 Charts Explain Exactly How Americans Spend $52 Billion on Our Pets in a Year." *Atlantic*, February 13, 2013. http://www.theatlantic.com/business/archive/2013/02/these-4-charts-explain-exactly-how-americans-spend-52-billion-on-our-pets-in-a-year/273446/.

Tolkien, J. R. R. *The Fellowship of the Ring.* New York: Houghton Mifflin Company, 1954.

UN. "Fast Facts: The Faces of Poverty." *Millennium Project.* 2006. (Accessed March 26, 2013). http://www.unmillenniumproject. org/documents/3-MP-PovertyFacts-E.pdf.

UNDP. *Cambodia Human Development Report 2007: Expanding Choices for Rural People.* http://hdr.undp.org/ en/reports/national/asiathepacific/cambodia/Cambodia_ HDR_2007.pdf.

US Department of State. *Trafficking in Persons Report 2012.* June 2012. http://www.state.gov/j/tip/rls/tiprpt/2012/.

Walk Free Foundation. "The Global Slavery Index 2014." Global Slavery Index. (Accessed February 17, 2015). http:// www.globalslaveryindex.org/.

Walker, Dinah. "Trends in U.S. Military Spending." Council on Foreign Relations. July 15, 2014. http://www.cfr.org/ defense-budget/trends-us-military-spending/p28855.

Wytsma, Ken. *Pursuing Justice.* Nashville: Thomas Nelson, 2013.

ACKNOWLEDGEMENTS

My journey as a writer, as a humanitarian, and as a person seeking my purpose is one where many people have walked beside me. A huge thanks to all those who have been a part of this project in big and small ways.

To the teachers who took my writing seriously from an early age—Mrs. Kirk, Mrs. Desnoyers, Mrs. Raine, and Mr. Kaminski: I'm grateful you saw something in me that was worth your time and investment. Thanks for your gentle criticisms, your enthusiasm, and your encouragement to pursue writing as a passion and a profession.

To the folks at Fools and Horses, the Fyxx, Roca House, and any other coffee house I frequented to write this book: Thanks for the great fair trade coffee, for the space for me to write this book, and for not kicking me out during those longer writing sessions. And on that note, thanks to the musical genius of M83, Daughter, Young Oceans, The XX, The National, Future of Forestry, Kye Kye, Angels and Airwaves, Coldplay, and other brilliant musicians who provided the tracks to my go-to playlist as I wrote this book.

Thanks to all my friends who have ever encouraged me to write and to keep writing. Thanks especially to Sarah, my biggest fan, my road-trip warrior, my partner in crime, my best friend—you've been there with me through thick and thin, even loving me at my darkest times. To Jay, Justin, Allison B.,

Cailey and Kyle, Allison M. and Paul, Jess C., and Kevin: You have all been key players in the opportunities, adventures, and discoveries I needed to experience in order to write this book. Thank you for your love, your support, and your insights and for celebrating every writing milestone with me.

To Keturah, my friend, my colleague, my brilliant editor and muse, my soul sister: Thank you for your gentle friendship, tough love, and deep support. Thank you for the countless hours of providing feedback on my work and your encouragement for me to write from the heart. This book has your imprints all over it. It would've been impossible without you.

Most of all, thanks to my family—the ones who first saw the writer in me before I could write, the ones who never gave up on drawing it out of me. To my parents for the precious gift of life and for the love of it: You gave me every opportunity I needed to be where I am today. As unqualified as I felt to take on this project, you've supported me from the very beginning. To my sister and lifelong friend, Kristy: Thank you for being the kind of sister who manages to be unfailingly protective and nurturing while also helping me to find my own set of wings. I've learned so much from you through your grace, patience, and wisdom. Thanks for having some of the most significant conversations and moments of my life with me.

This journey has been difficult and messy, and I've been ready to give up more than once. But because of all of you and your support along the way, it's also been beautiful and renewing, and I wouldn't trade it—or any of you—for anything. Thank you!

CPSIA information can be obtained
at www.ICGtesting.com
Printed in the USA
LVOW12s1117200217
524806LV00001B/159/P